The Freelance Content Marketing Writer

Find your perfect clients,
Make tons of money and
Build a business you love

JENNIFER GOFORTH GREGORY

The Freelance Content Marketing Writer
Find your perfect clients, make tons of money, and build a business you love

ISBN: 978-1-7322409-0-2
Cover and interior design by Nehmen-Kodner: n-kcreative.com
Printed in the United States of America
Published by Jennifer Goforth Gregory
JenniferGregoryWriter.com

Contents

INTRODUCTION

A re you a freelance journalist looking to move into content marketing to increase your income? Do you want to leave a full-time job to become a freelancer? Maybe you worked in the media or marketing industry before kids and want to freelance now that the little ones are starting school. Perhaps you are currently writing freelance content marketing for clients but want to grow your business. If so, then you've picked up the right book. I can help you achieve your goals.

This book is for anyone who is a competent writer and wants to build or grow a content marketing writing business. You don't have to be the world's best writer—you just need to be a good writer, love writing and be willing to learn how to tailor your writing to the client's needs. I describe a step-by-step approach that can be used by people who are starting a freelance business from scratch or by current freelancers wanting to grow their business. Regardless of your experience with writing and freelancing, this book will help you get from where you are to where you want to be.

The strategies in this book really work. These aren't just things that I made up in my head and hope will work, but this book is a road map of exactly how I've built and grown my business over the years. And over the past five years I've gotten hundreds of emails from other writers who read my blog telling me the successes that they've seen from following my advice—new clients, breaking six figures, being able to quit their jobs to freelance full-time. In many ways, each of those emails means more to me than any amount of money I've earned. And I have the faith that you too can have the very same level of success. I hope to see a happy email in my inbox from you in the near future.

Why I Wrote This Book

It was 2008. My youngest kid was heading to kindergarten and I decided to launch a freelance business so I could have the flexibility I wanted as a mom. And also, so I didn't have to go back to my boring full-time job as a technical writer, updating the same software manuals until the end of time. I figured that I could just start a freelancing business and I would be instantly successful. I had the experience, I had the ability and I really wanted it to work.

But it didn't happen that way. Not even close.

On my way back from dropping my son off at his first day of kindergarten, I bought a copy of *Writer's Market* and got to work. I pitched and got crickets. I applied for more freelance gigs than I thought were possible. I wrote very low-paying gigs for content mills. And I spent my days writing about anything that someone would pay to write about—from golf to weddings to health—you name it, I probably wrote about it, and for $25 an article.

Then slowly I got some traction, but not like I had envisioned. It wasn't the big-time newspapers or the glossy magazines that I paged through while checking out at Target. I published a few stories in local magazines. Then I published a story in a Kentucky parenting magazine. Over the next few years, I was published in regional parenting magazines in towns I'd never heard of. And then eventually I began writing stories for a local newspaper for what I thought was big money at $75 a story. I just kept cranking along taking whatever I could get.

This went on for four years. And I never broke $30K a single year even though I was working full-time.

Then one day in early 2011, I applied to a job posted by a content marketing company and got put on a project. I didn't have any idea what content marketing was—I just knew it was a step up from what I had been doing. I kept moving forward. An editor liked the seemingly 34 million blog posts I wrote about how to make webinars interesting and put me on a new project—American Express OPEN Forum. And things started to change for my career and my bank account.

Content was just becoming a thing about the same time I figured out that what I was spending my days (and many nights) writing actually had a name. I started marketing myself as a content marketing writer and one gig turned into another—IBM, Intuit, Costco, Allstate, State Farm. I broke $50K and felt like I had earned a million dollars. About that time, I started my blog (in the spring of 2013) to help other writers do the same thing. I have spent the past five years trying to share what has worked for me with other writers while also learning a ton from my readers at the same time.

I kept plugging away. I developed a niche and started marketing myself better. I started figuring out what type of clients were most likely to hire me. I started landing some great clients—Adobe, Samsung, Hewlett Packard, Verizon—some direct and some through agencies. Then the next year I doubled my income to break six figures for the first time.

Even though I've stayed at the six-figure level for the past three years, success isn't something you hit once and are set for life. Freelancing is a constant roller coaster. I've been fired by clients, made embarrassing typos and went through a period of no paying work. Even last week I lost a client because they didn't think I was a fit for the project anymore, and I came to a very rational conclusion at 3 a.m. that I was a complete fraud and needed to change careers.

But after spending all night fretting, I got up, drank several Diet Mountain Dews and got to work putting the exact same strategies I'm going to share with you into play. And within two days, I had four new assignments with existing clients, a brand-new project for a ginormous company and two calls scheduled the next week with two potential clients. Everything I share with you in this book really works, regardless of whether you are just starting out or have been freelancing for years but hit a dry spell.

However, you aren't going to get to six figures or even a smaller increase next week or next month. It takes time. It takes persistence and you must believe you can do it. While I have definitely had my share of 3 a.m. career crises, I have never really doubted my ability to be a successful freelancer. On the tough days, I remind myself that other writers are making real money, so why can't I do it also?

You Must Be Persistent and Believe in Yourself

I'm going to show you how to build and grow a business that you love, based on your very unique set of experiences, skills and strengths. But you are going to need to bring an extraordinary level of persistence, also known as stubbornness. You are also going to need to really believe in your heart that you can do this, that you can meet your earning goals and be successful freelancer. I will give you tips and ideas on how to do this, but ultimately, the persistence and a strong belief in yourself is going to have to come from you.

How to Use This Book

This isn't the type of book that you read, get inspired and go back to your regularly scheduled life. You will only reach your goals if you put in the work. This book contains a lot of information and tips, which can be overwhelming. To help you pick which areas to focus on based on your specific situation, I've included four different personalized road maps in the Appendix that point you to the tasks that are most applicable to help you get started on the strategies for your career stage and goals.

Throughout this book, I've added Build Your Business exercises with practical steps for you to take. Some of these are questions to ask yourself to chart your course, others are specific actions like updating your website with your niches, and a few involve taking an honest look at your business. I recommend doing these as you read the book or at least after finishing each chapter. If you are the type to read ahead—no judgment, I'm the same—then be sure to come back and look for the Build Your Business icons.

Throughout the book, I talk about the importance of networking with other writers. An easy way to do this is to join the Freelance Content Marketing Writer Facebook group. You can ask any questions you have about the book, share your successes and get encouragement on the tough days. I also recommend visiting my blog jennifergregorywriter.com/blog and subscribing to my newsletter so you can get the latest post each week delivered to your email.

You Can Do This

It is very possible to make six figures as a freelancer. Many other writers are making this type of money and there is no reason why you can't as well.

While it's easy to feel like you are the only one experiencing challenges as a freelancer, that is the furthest thing from the truth. Every freelancer experiences highs and lows and days where they convince themselves they are a fraud, no matter if they are just starting out or been doing this for 20 years. You are not alone.

The good news is that if you already have experience writing professionally, either as a journalist or marketer, then you already have the majority of the skills needed to be a successful content marketing writer. If you bring the persistence and truly believe that you can do this, I can guide you through the rest of the lessons so you can increase your income as a content marketing writer.

You can do this. I promise.

Section 1: Before You Get Started

You will note that much to my editor's chagrin, I use the term *content marketing* throughout this book instead of *content*. Yes, I know it's a mouthful, but I made the conscious choice to use this particular phrase. Many freelance writers, especially journalists, dislike the term *content marketing* because it includes the term *marketing*. And writers often feel that marketing doesn't really describe the heavily reported and well-written story that they created for a brand.

I get this. I really do. But this is the thing: the people who are looking to hire you use the term content marketing. And if we as writers use another term like *branded content*, *custom content*, *content* or *brand journalism*, it just makes it harder for people who need our skills to find us. Using the words *content marketing* doesn't make our work less valuable or mean we are selling out. Yes, I don't like the term *content marketing* either because I don't think it accurately reflects the high level of writing that often goes into these stories. But I feel very strongly that writers need to use the same terminology used by the people who hire us.

So, with that out of the way, let's dive in and talk about content marketing. Even if you have been writing content marketing for years, I highly recommend reading (or at least skimming) this section. Yes, I know, I'm the type to sneak to the last page of a book. But this section covers some basics that we will build throughout the rest of the book.

Chapter 1

What Is Content Marketing Writing?

Content marketing is when a business provides information to its potential customers that helps solve their problems. It can be in the form of a blog post, video, iPhone app, whitepaper, even a webinar or event. The business offers interesting, relevant and useful content that inspires the readers (target customers) to develop trust in the brand, which is the ultimate goal. And then when the readers/customers go to make a purchasing decision, they will already have a relationship with the business and be more likely to purchase their products or services.

If you find the term confusing, you are not alone. The word marketing makes people think that content marketing is something different from what it really is. To help give a clearer picture, here are five types of writing projects that fall under the umbrella of content marketing:

- An article in an airline magazine about a travel destination
- A blog post with a recipe for a cake cooked in a slow cooker on a blog produced by a slow cooker manufacturer
- A newsletter a hospital sends to people living nearby with tips and information about staying healthy
- An alumni magazine sent to alumni of the university

- An association magazine sent to members of the association
- Ghostwritten content for experts and executives, such as articles and blog posts

On the flip side, here are a few projects that are marketing instead of content marketing because they do not provide non-product or company information that is interesting or helps solve problems. All of the information in these projects revolve around the company and products:

- Website copy about products
- Case studies written by a brand
- Press release
- Product one-sheets
- Advertorials about a company or product

Many companies make the mistake of creating content with the purpose of selling their products and talking about how great they are. This just doesn't work. Effective content marketing is when the content produced simply addresses the needs of the target customer with very few (if any) mentions of the company's products or services. In fact, most pieces of great content could appear in newspapers, consumer pubs, trade pubs, or online pubs with few or no changes. My favorite examples include American Express OPEN Forum, airline magazines and *Costco Connection* magazine. All of these provide journalistic-style content with the goal of helping customers and building trust. The information in these websites and publications is almost identical to stories found in top consumer publications.

While sometimes people call content marketing writing "copywriting" because it is created for corporate clients, there is a difference. Content marketing is creating information that is not product/brand focused. The main purpose is providing information. Copywriting is creating content centered around products and services, such as brochures, sales sheets and landing pages. The primary intent is to sell.

Who Hires Content Marketing Writers?

You may be surprised at how many types of businesses use—or could use—content marketing writing. Here is an overview of the types of clients that hire content marketing writers.

• **Brands.** A great way to earn top dollar and see the impact of your content marketing is to write directly for a company. One type of company sells products or services to consumers, referred to as B2C (Business-to-Consumer), which includes hotels, food & beverage, retailers of all kinds and pretty much any type of company that sells products. The other type is B2B (Business-to-Business), which are companies selling products and services to other companies, such as technology products, expert services such as consulting, and IT and any specialty items needed for the business. Some examples are businesses that sell project management software, companies making medical equipment for doctors and dentists, companies selling high-power printers to *businesses*. B2B is an especially lucrative market for content marketing writers because you must be familiar with the industry, so there are fewer writers in these areas, meaning you can command higher rates.

• **Content Marketing/Public Relations (PR) Firms.** Public relations firms are increasingly finding themselves being asked to produce content for customers and often need additional writers. One of my most steady clients is a technology PR firm that has hired for a variety of deliverables, including case studies, blog posts and ghostwritten articles for major publications. One of the good things is that you can break into multiple industries and have steady work sent your way. On the flip side, some agencies pay lower because they take a cut of the client pay.

• **Content Companies.** I unknowingly began my career as a content marketing writer when I answered a job ad for Contently, a content marketing company. Companies such as Contently, Skyword, Ebyline (and others) provide content marketing writing and act as middlemen between the writers and the brands. Each company works differently with some providing editors and staffing the teams while others have the writers work directly with the brands. The pay ranges greatly based on the projects, as does the caliber of clients, but you typically make less going through a company than contracting directly with a brand.

• **Professionals.** It is essential that people trust their doctors, lawyers and financial planners. These professionals have a lot of information to share and providing content on their website can be a great way to both increase their search engine ranking and earn the trust of potential customers. Many professionals may not realize that they need help and have never worked with a writer, so it may take more marketing to land these clients.

• **Associations and Universities.** Most associations and universities publish a print magazine with information for their members and alumni. These magazines fall under content marketing since they contain content to further the brand (association or magazine). Also, many departments have their own publications as well as other needs for writers. Outside of the alumni magazine, it can be challenging to find the right people, but when you break into a university, you can often land lucrative and ongoing work.

• **Nonprofits.** The best way for nonprofits to raise money for their causes is to share the stories of the people that they have helped. Many nonprofits use freelance writers to craft these feature stories, which are often very journalistic in nature. While some nonprofits do pay lower fees, others are well funded and have healthy budgets.

• **Hospitals.** Most hospitals provide information to consumers to help them better manage their health with the purpose of increasing trust in the hospital. This content may be in the form of newsletters, emails or website content. Some hospitals provide information to doctors as well, which is also content marketing. Many hospitals outsource their content needs to agencies so sometimes it can take some sleuthing to find out who produces the newsletter and website content for your local hospitals.

What Do Content Marketing Writers Write?

Content marketing can be more than just blogs and articles, though. Content marketing also includes video, infographics and even trade show events. A great example of thinking outside the page for content marketing is the Zoës Kitchen L.I.F.E. app. In addition to tracking the fast-casual restaurant's loyalty program, the app helps customers measure progress on their lifestyle goals, such as exercise and healthy eating. Chipotle hosts a fantastic music event designed to educate people about clean eating and sustainable farming practices, and that event falls under the umbrella of content marketing as well.

While content can come in any form, there are certain types of deliverables that are more common than others. As a content marketing writer, you will most likely be hired to write the following:

• **Blogs.** A blog is the most common and by far the easiest way for a brand to launch their content marketing strategy. Businesses blog about topics that will help potential customers solve problems and become educated on their topic. The blog posts shouldn't be sales oriented but should be informative to the brand's potential customers. As a content marketing writer, you may also find yourself ghostwriting blog topics for a representative of the brand as well as writing unbylined blog posts.

• **Articles (Both Print and Online).** If a brand has a custom content magazine, such as *Costco Connection*, then you may write articles for the print magazine and/or the website, both of which educate customers and often highlight products. Other brands create an article library on their website, such as a cardiologist who drives potential patients to her website with articles on keeping your heart healthy. Content marketing writers may also ghostwrite articles, often for trade publications, for an executive of a brand.

• **Case Studies.** Case studies show potential customers how a brand's products can be used in real life to make a difference. These are typically used by B2B companies and are often a cross between feature writing and marketing writing. Case studies are often overlooked by brands but can be a great sales tool. For example, a technology company may create a case study on how a hotel used their property management system (software that manages all parts of the hotel) to increase guest satisfaction and revenue.

• **Whitepapers.** They are typically 4 to 10 pages long and provide insightful ideas and perspective on a topic, not just reporting but generating ideas. Be aware that some companies call a piece of content a whitepaper when really it is a sales brochure. Great whitepapers focus on ideas, not the product.

• **Infographics.** Infographics are all the rage these days. Effective infographics are not just a cool image, but they actually tell a story, typically by breaking down the issue into bite-sized facts. Since graphic design and writing are different skill sets (and only a few lucky people possess both), most companies use writers to craft the text and a graphic designer to make the content eye-catching.

• **Video Scripts.** In recent years, Content Marketing Institute (CMI) reports have shown that video is one of the biggest areas of increase in content. Each video needs a script. Many writers overlook video, but it can be a very lucrative market.

• **E-books.** Many companies offer e-books either free or for a nominal charge to provide information to potential customers. They can be a very effective form of content marketing, but e-books are time-consuming so are a perfect deliverable to hire a freelancer to write.

New Terms to Learn

Marketers use different terms than journalists or even other business people. And yes, you are going to be exposed to a ton of jargon. Here are a few words that you are likely to hear on content marketing projects:

• **B2B (Business-to-Business)** – Refers to a company that markets their products for businesses to use as opposed to consumers. A company selling software to insurance agencies is B2B.

• **B2C (Business-to-Consumer)** – This type of company sells stuff directly to consumers, such as clothing, soda, food and all of the other things we buy.

• **Content Strategy** – A plan for your content marketing that includes your purpose, type of content, what you want to accomplish, where you will publish the content, social media strategy and metrics to measure the success of the content.

• **Persona** – A mock-up character that represents one of the users of the products. Marketers usually give personas funny names and write a little bio that includes both demographic information as well as more interesting details like what keeps them up at night and what magazines they read. As a writer, you may be given a persona and asked to write your content to that persona.

• **Deliverable** – Refers to the finished product, such as the blog post, article, video or infographic text.

• **SME (Subject Matter Expert)** – A person who is an expert on a topic and typically going to provide you with information you need to create the content. To make this one even more fun, it's usually pronounced "SMEEEE."

• **CTA (Call to Action)** – This is a few sentences at the bottom of a piece of content that refers the reader to another piece of content, such as a company website or a specific whitepaper. Often, it's the only reference to a company on a piece of content.

• **Thought Leadership** – This used to mean a piece of content that provides new and original ideas. And that's what I think it really SHOULD mean. But I've been hearing more people use it lately to mean content that doesn't mention the product.

Often thought leadership means a piece that is ghostwritten for someone, often an executive.

• **Sales Funnel** – This is really a fancy way of referring to the different stages that customers go through before they buy a product. While it may seem simple for buying consumer products like a candy bar, it's really complex in the B2B world because it involves a lot of steps and people. Clients will often tell you that you are writing a piece of content at a specific sales funnel stage. The majority of the content I work on is at the Awareness stage, which means you are trying to get people to trust the company by providing great information that makes their life easier. Typically, whitepapers and case studies are further down the funnel, such as at the Decision stage. Content that is read at the top of the funnel is typically less focused on the brand and product, meaning it's more journalistic in style. The closer you get to the bottom, the more the content tends to move away from content marketing towards marketing.

• **Stakeholders** – You may hear a client say, "I need to run this by the stakeholders." That basically means all the people who care about the piece of content. It usually means everyone who has to sign off on the content, but not always. If you want to impress a client use this term in your initial conversation and ask to have all stakeholders sign off on both the outline and first draft to reduce revisions.

• **ROI (Return on Investment)** – This term is used to describe how much money the company will make from a particular investment. For example, if a business spent $3,000 on a whitepaper, but the deliverable (yes, I did that on purpose) was downloaded 200 times and resulted in five businesses purchasing a total of $17,000 in software then the gain on the original investment was $14,000. That's an ROI of 467 percent. Many companies are currently looking to determine how effective their content marketing dollars are and ROI is the way that they often track the results of their strategy.

You May Already Be a Content Marketing Writer

Have you ever written an article for an airline magazine? How about an association publication? Maybe AARP? Perhaps you have written for an alumni magazine or three? Or you wrote for a hospital newsletter or magazine? If so, then you have actually already written content marketing. All of these types of publications fall into the realm of content marketing because they are produced by brands or organizations for customers or potential customers.

You are most likely either cringing or smiling at this moment. Writers who have purposely avoided content marketing writing are usually shocked and a bit disconcerted to find out that many of the publications that they considered journalism are actually content. And on the flip side, writers wanting to break into content are thrilled that they actually have experience. Many people are surprised that content isn't a new thing, just a new name for a type of writing that many of us have written for years (or decades).

Content marketing strategy includes the same deliverables and same objectives that many of us have been writing for corporate clients for many years. But now these projects fall under the umbrella of content marketing, and companies are giving higher priority to them. If you have written any of these types of deliverables, then you already have experience as a content marketing writer:

- Blog posts for a business
- Newsletter article with informative articles (not just promotional)
- Articles for custom publication for businesses or associations
- Alumni publications
- Airline magazines
- Whitepapers
- Case studies

Is Content Marketing Going to Go Away Soon?

Content marketing has been a hot trend for years. Over the past few months, I have heard and read writers discussing their concerns about the content marketing work drying up. Will the same thing happen to content as happened in recent years to consumer pubs with the opportunities being less and less?

I called my friend Stephanie in a panic. Was content marketing going away? Had I built my career on something trendy and unsustainable? As you will see throughout the book, Stephanie is a very good friend and spends a lot of time talking me off ledges. She told me that she had been writing content marketing for 20 years, but it used to be referred to as custom publications, meaning magazines produced by brands. And then custom content evolved into content marketing. And that, no, content marketing by some name or form would always be around.

As usual, she was 100 percent right. Yes, in five years what we call content marketing today will likely evolve into something else with a different name and some different nuances. But companies are always going to need writers to create information for their customers. And as long as the internet is around, businesses are going to need freelancer writers to create information for their customers. I think that this is especially true for writers with specialized niches.

But that also means as a freelance content marketing writer, you need to keep an eye out for new trends and keep your skills up-to-date. You want to make sure when the next evolution of what is now content marketing happens, you can easily make the transition. I am currently doing this by trying to get experience using video and creating interactive content. But it's very possible that the next version of custom content/content marketing will be totally unrelated.

(!) **Build Your Business:** Take 15 minutes to go through articles and blogs that you have previously written (also known as your clips) and see what projects you have written that now fall under the term "content marketing." If you are an experienced freelancer, you probably have more content marketing writing experience than you think you do.

KEY TAKEAWAYS:
What Is Content Marketing Writing?

- Content marketing is providing interesting and relevant information to potential customers.

- If something looks and smells like marketing, then it is not content marketing—it is just plain marketing.

- Association publications (AARP), airline magazines, alumni magazines, and magazines produced by companies (*Costco Connection*) are content marketing.

- In addition to blogs, content marketing includes infographic text, video scripts and e-books along with many other types of projects.

Chapter 2

Journalists and Content Marketing

If you are currently writing journalism and want to add content marketing writing to your services, then this chapter is specifically for you. If you are currently mainly writing content or starting from scratch to build a content business, then skip this chapter and go to chapter 3.

It's hard to make a good living by writing only freelance journalism these days due to publications going out of business, shrinking magazines and lower rates. Many freelance journalists are now turning to content marketing to increase their income and find a way to support their families as freelancers.

Four Key Similarities between Journalism and Content Marketing Writing

Content marketing writing is very similar to journalism in many ways. People tend to focus on the differences, but the skills that make someone a fantastic journalist can also make you a successful content marketing writer.

• **Solid writing is the cornerstone.** With both types of writing, you need to write solid pieces that are grammatically correct, clear, concise and accurate. No matter the deliverable, client or audience, you must provide your clients with well-written content.

• **Sourcing and interviewing are key.** The right source is often the difference between an okay piece of writing and a great one. This is true in both content marketing and traditional journalism. Finding the right source brings authority and credibility to your writing. And if you are able to get great quotes, your readers will be more engaged in what you are saying.

• **There is an editing process.** It's very rare that you will send a story to a consumer or trade publication and the editor does not make changes. The same is true with content marketing deliverables. As with traditional journalism, a great editor will work with a writer to create an even stronger piece.

• **Understanding the publication/brand is instrumental to success.** Editors love writers who make their jobs easier, especially ones who come up with interesting story ideas that are a fit for their publication or brand. I have found that I often get repeat assignments simply because I shoot off a quick pitch to editors with whom I previously worked, showing that I understand their audiences' needs.

Six Key Differences between Content Marketing Writing and Journalism

I've had a number of conversations in the past few years with veteran journalists who are frustrated. These writers have years in the field. Their clips are full of prestigious publications. But they can't figure out how to break into content marketing. Or they feel they have missed the boat on content marketing. A few mentioned that they just don't think they have the skills needed to move into content marketing.

This is the thing—you already have all the skills you need and you are definitely not too late. Content marketing isn't something huge and different. It's just a slight shift from what you have been doing successfully for years.

But you do need to be aware of a few differences when considering writing content marketing.

1. The purpose of content marketing writing is to increase trust in your client's brand.

If you write an article for a consumer or trade publication, your purpose is to educate or entertain readers so they will continue to purchase the magazine. With content marketing, the purpose of all your deliverables is to provide valuable content to the reader to establish the brand's expertise in the industry. If done correctly, this increases the amount of trust that the potential customer has for the brand. While this is a subtle difference, you must keep it at the front of your mind because it affects everything from subtle messaging within text to topics to even allowable sources.

2. Your client is a brand instead of a publication.

When you write for a traditional publication, you are hired by the publication to write the article or blog post. However, when you write content marketing materials, your client is the brand. Some content marketing writers work through a content company such as Contently, Skyword or Ebyline, but even in that case, their end client is still the brand.

3. You have to know more about your audience than in journalism.

Knowing your audience is a skill that writers have been focusing on since the beginning of time. But with content marketing writing, it is even more important and your audience is typically much better defined. Often, it is a specific niche within a company's target demographic that they are looking to capitalize on. It is important to understand your audience's needs, problems and sources of information.

4. You have to write in the brand voice.
In journalism, you can use your own voice. In fact, most publications want you to use your own style and voice. In content marketing, you have to use the brand voice, which can be a big challenge. Brand voice is the tone that companies use when talking to the customer and can vary a lot based on company. I honestly think this is the hardest part of content marketing. For example, IBM is going to use a different tone when talking to their customers than Patagonia. As a writer this means that you have to use a different tone for each client. But it can be challenging to get the tone exactly right. I will talk about how to get the right tone in chapter 9.

5. You can't directly compare journalism rates and content marketing rates.
Many journalists use $1 per word as their benchmark for determining whether an assignment is worth taking. But in content marketing you can miss jobs that pay well by using a per-word benchmark. You have to go by the hourly rate that you will earn instead. That does not mean you will charge $50 an hour to write the piece. It means that you will get a project fee that works out to, say, 50 cents per word, but you have to do less work to earn it, so overall you can come out ahead. For example, if a magazine assigns you a 1,000-word piece for $1 per word and it takes you a total of 25 hours to pitch the piece, locate and interview sources, write the piece and revise per the editor's comments, then you have earned a rate of $40 an hour ($1,000 divided by 25). But if a content marketing client assigns you 1,000 words for a flat fee of $600 (60 cents per word) and it takes you only 12

hours to write the piece (since the client provides all necessary materials), then you have earned a fee of $50 per hour, which better compensates you for the actual time it took to write the piece. The client typically gives you assignments or asks for short pitches (a sentence or two on a specific topic). This takes much less time and has a dramatically higher success rate than cold pitches to publication editors. When clients give you an assignment, they often give you the source and contact information. I've even had clients give me transcripts or an approved outline.

If you are working with an agency, they usually handle the majority of the client interaction, which saves time as well. Often there is less work involved for a content marketing project, meaning you will spend less time on the project, resulting in a higher hourly rate. I will talk about setting rates in great detail in chapter 13.

6. You must identify a niche and sell yourself as an expert in this niche.
As a journalist, you can write on almost any topic of interest to you. But in content marketing, you need to develop a niche in order to be able to write quickly and well. I will explain the reasons and exactly how to find your niches in detail in chapter 3. You may think you don't have a niche, but you do. I am positive that if you go through your clips, you will find many subjects that you have written on many times over the years. You may have a certain beat that could be turned into a niche.

None of these concepts or topics are new to freelance writers. Each one is simply a twist or a different emphasis on something that we are already doing all day long. While there are definitely some small differences, I am positive that any freelance writer or journalist who wants to add content marketing to their services already has the majority of the expertise they need to be successful.

Can You Ethically Write Content Marketing and Journalism?

Because content marketing writing represents a brand, and journalism is supposed to be unbiased, some writers are concerned that they cannot ethically do both. Can you write *for* Microsoft as a content marketing writer and then write *about* Microsoft for the *New York Times*? Probably not. Even if you are strictly fair and impartial in the *Times* piece, the perception that you might have a conflict of interest is enough to make the *Times* editors break out in hives.

But that doesn't mean you must turn in your journalism hat the moment you write your first content marketing piece. Many writers, including myself, successfully straddle this line. While I am sure that there are some writers making a high income writing only journalism, I have found that most of the writers who earn six figures and above write a combination of journalism and content.

In my experience—both personal and talking to other writers—the vast majority of editors do not care if you write both content and journalism, especially in different niches. In full disclosure, though, a very small handful of publications (such as some editors at the *New York Times* and *Wall Street Journal*) will not use writers who have written custom content. If you are currently writing for these publications or hope to write for these publications, you should take this into consideration before jumping into content. However, different editors have different stances on this issue, so it's not cut-and-dried.

But you do have to put thought into your client choices and consciously consider potential conflicts of interest.

Keeping separate niches in content marketing and journalism is a good first step. For example, you can write content marketing in the automotive industry and do travel journalism. This keeps things pretty neat and clean. However, many writers are able to do both within the same niche, especially in large niches like business, tech and finance.

To help myself navigate these waters, I came up with some personal guidelines. Here are my three rules for writing both content marketing and journalism:

1. Never use someone you have taken money from as a source. This rule is the cornerstone of doing both content and journalism. If a client hires you to create content for a brand and then you later use the client as a source in a story, it could easily be perceived that you used them as a source only because they are your client. When I take a client, I think long and hard about how it will impact my ability to write journalistic stories in the future that could involve that client.

2. Disclose any possible conflicts of interest before working on any project.
This is key to writing both content marketing and journalism. If there are any potential conflicts, tell both the brand and the publication before you start work. If there is an iota of a chance that someone else could *perceive* a conflict, have the conversation. I have had many of these conversations and have found that the editors almost always say it's no issue. And even if they do have a concern, I always earn brownie points up front for having the conversation.

3. Do not place articles for a client in a journalistic publication.
A client may ask you to write an article about their company and then pitch it to the publications that you write for as a journalistic article, with you getting paid by both the company and the

publication. This is absolutely unethical. But clients ask quite often so you have to be prepared for it.

Sometimes you follow the guidelines you made for your business and it still doesn't seem right. I had been working for a hospitality trade publication for years and was offered a content gig to write about hospitality technology for a very large electronics company. Everyone was fine with me doing both, but after a few months, I just didn't feel good about it so I decided to no longer write for the trade publication.

Rules are great. Lines in the sand are needed. But sometimes even when you follow everything that you have decided to do, you still have a funny feeling. You know the nagging voice in your head. Or maybe it's a queasy feeling in your stomach that lets you know something feels off. Even if it seems ethical, but your gut says no, then my advice is to listen to your gut, 100 percent of the time. No paycheck or byline is worth compromising your integrity or your ethics.

KEY TAKEAWAYS:
Journalists and Content Marketing

• If a brand hires you as a freelancer, then you cannot ethically use anyone at a company as a source for a journalism story in the future.

• Journalists already have most of the skills—finding sources, interviewing sources and writing a great story—needed to be successful freelancers.

• Writing in the brand voice is usually the hardest part of moving from journalism to content marketing.

• Consider having separate niches for content marketing and journalism to avoid conflicts.

Section 2: Find Your Perfect Client

The best part about content marketing is that every business is a potential client. Pretty much every business needs content to attract clients these days. While this is a very good thing, it also makes it very hard for writers to know how to find clients. Unlike journalism, you can't go into a bookstore or do a Google search for publications. Instead, you have to figure out exactly which clients are likely to hire you based on your specific experience and expertise. Then get those clients to hire you.

This section guides you through this process from start to finish. If you take the time to do the Build Your Business exercises in these chapters, you will have a list of potential clients and a Letter of Introduction (LOI) to use to contact these clients. Since the perfect client and perfect LOI are unique for each writer, you really must go through the exercises one by one to get to the point of making a high income.

Yes, it will take some time. But building a business that you love doesn't happen overnight. And it doesn't happen by waiting for someone to offer you work. You must find the confidence to go out and convince people that you are the writer that they have been waiting for. There are companies and agencies out there right now who are looking to hire writers with your expertise and experience. You just have to help them find you.

Chapter 3

Find Your Niches

Several years ago, an editor asked me if I had experience writing about pets and offered me a very well-paying gig. I sent her a few clips I'd written on dogs and cats. I was excited to write about something outside my typical area of technology and was thrilled when she hired me. My blog posts about keeping the litter box clean and house-training your puppy sailed through. But everything changed when I started writing about fish.

While I am not a fish expert, I honestly thought I knew enough to write about fish—we have several fish tanks in our house and I know how to research new topics. But I quickly realized that fish are far more technical than I could have imagined. I spent many hours researching the topics only to have the editor not like anything I wrote. My hourly rate was less than I would have earned working at the local drive-thru, the client was irritated and I was embarrassed. I lost the client and vowed never to write about fish again.

For the next year or so, I stayed within my niches and all was good. But then one day the editor of a lifestyle blog for an insurance company asked me to write some lifestyle pieces. I was already doing work on insurance topics for another blog for the company. "Sure, no problem," I told the editor. And thought to myself, How hard can it be to write about home and garden stuff? I mean, I have a home and I love to garden. Famous last words.

It was a disaster. I spent over 20 hours on a 500-word post about building a fire pit, had four rounds of revisions and the legal department ended up getting involved because of risk of someone burning down their house based on my directions. It got so bad that my writer friend Stephanie offered to just fix my story so that she didn't have to hear me whining about it anymore. And the worst part was that I lost my great gig with the other blog on insurance, all because I stepped outside of my niche.

I finally said to my writer friends, "I'm not going to write about lifestyle stuff anymore. I'm going to stick to easy topics like data analytics, cloud computing and internet security." Yes, to most people this seems absurd since the majority of writers find lifestyle topics much easier than technology. But that is the thing—niches are very specific to each person and writers should focus on their specific strengths, not what they think is lucrative or easy for other writers.

What Exactly Is a Niche?

A niche is a topic area where you are knowledgeable about the industry, have a solid understanding of the needs of the potential customer base, are up-to-date on the trends and have connections with industry experts. It's not something that you've written about a few times or watched a documentary on, but a topic on which you have actual knowledge and expertise.

When I attend conferences, other writers ask me for tips about breaking into content marketing writing or finding more work. And as always, the first question I'm asked when I meet marketing professionals is "What is your niche?" And my answer is "I'm a finance writer" or "I write about health." While this answer is fine for casual conversation in the halls of a writers' conference, I promise that you will get more work if you reframe this answer both in your own head and for clients.

The first step is to stop thinking of your writing in broad terms such as a technology, health, finance, food, travel or whatever other general subject you've been using to identify your writing. You need to dig deeper in your niche and think of it in terms as specific as possible. Within your niche, what specific areas do you consider yourself an expert? For what topics do you truly understand the audience needs? And for what subjects within the broader niche do you have clips or work experience to prove your expertise?

So instead of "I'm a health writer," you should think of yourself as a dental implant, neurology, or gluten-free nutrition writer. If you are in finance, then maybe you are a college planning, credit card or Roth IRA writer. You can have as many niches within your larger niche as you want, but the more specific you are, the better. I honestly don't think you can be too specific. As long as there are companies that market to that particular audience, then it's a great niche.

I have broad niches, such as technology, but also have specific areas within technology where I have significant experience, such as Voice over Internet Protocol (VoIP), data analytics and Internet of Things. If I am approaching a company that needs someone who understands and writes about a variety of types of technology topics, then I will market myself as a technology writer. But if someone needs a telecommunications writer then the subject line of my LOI reads "Experienced VoIP Content Marketing Writer." My income increased greatly once I started marketing myself this way during networking events, on my LinkedIn profile, on my website and in LOIs.

If you are new at freelancing and wondering what in the world you can use for a niche, don't despair. Even if you do not have clips in your niche, you have considerable expertise in many areas either from previous jobs, hobbies or life experience (being a parent, owning a dog, buying a house). And you can absolutely use these to create a niche. Later in this chapter, I give more ideas of how to find your niches even if you don't have clips.

The Importance of Having a Niche

I used to think that I could write about almost any topic. As a journalist for the local newspaper, I did write about pretty much any topic. It was just a matter of doing some research, finding great sources, asking the right questions and then pulling it all together in a story. So when I moved to content marketing, I assumed the same steps would apply. But I have learned (the very hard way) that when it comes to content marketing, this is not true.

Here are three reasons I recommend having a niche or many niches for content marketing writing:

1. With content marketing writing, you need to write from a place of authority, so you need to understand the topic and the audience.
Much of content marketing writing is actually thought leadership, where you are writing unique ideas and positions about trends and solutions to a problem. Instead of telling someone else's story and using quotes from sources (as is typical when writing for consumer or trade publications), you create the story from new ideas based on prior knowledge. This can be a big challenge for people transitioning from journalism. I explain more about how to do this in chapter 9.

2. It is more difficult to get gigs as a content marketing writer while marketing yourself as a generalist without areas of specialty.
This is especially true with agencies since their clients want writers with expertise in their industry. When I attended Content Marketing World, a large conference for content marketing professionals, for the first time in 2015, the first question that every person asked after I introduced myself as a freelancer was "What do you write about?" Many of these people were interested in hiring a freelancer, but their primary concern was niches, not just writing ability.

3. Having a niche makes it easier to identify potential clients.
The good news and the bad news about content marketing is that the number of potential clients is limitless. Instead of the huge number of possible clients making marketing myself easier, I have found it makes marketing myself more difficult. If you think in terms of being a health writer, then you have pretty much the entire medical community to market yourself to, which often makes writers feel paralyzed. But if you are a dental implant writer, then your potential clients are now implant dentists and all the companies that produce products that implant dentists use in their practice—a narrower niche narrows down your prospective list as well.

You also have a much higher chance of getting the job with a narrow focus. There are a TON of technology writers. Technology, just like health, has a wide range—from people who write about mobile phone apps to the really geeky stuff like how to recover from a ransomware attack if your company uses a virtualized network. When I marketed myself as just a technology writer, I didn't stand out from the crowd very much (and didn't get much work). But my income skyrocketed as soon as

I began specializing (and marketing myself accordingly) with a highlight on my expertise in data analytics and cloud computing. Because, not surprisingly, there are not a million people who call themselves data analytics content marketing writers.

Many writers are resistant to niches because they don't want to write about the same thing every day. One of the biggest perks of being a freelancer is writing and learning about a variety of different topics. But the great news is that you can have as many niches as you want. I have about eight different niches. Some are related, such as personal finance and credit cards. But others represent a wide range, including hotel technology, social media, cloud computing and cable television.

The trick is, when marketing myself to a specific company, I present myself like that industry is my main focus and that I am an expert in that area. For example, when offering my services to a B2B company, I will write that I specialize in content marketing for small businesses. But if I am replying to a mortgage company looking for content, then I will include my personal finance clips.

Can Generalists Land Content Marketing Gigs?

Yes. Absolutely. Without a doubt. I know many high-income content marketing writers that are generalists. I find that most writers I know who say they are generalists typically have several (if not more) niches—it's just that the niches are usually unrelated. And the writers like to have the freedom to write about whatever they want without feeling locked into a niche. This is totally fine and a great way to make an income without being bored.

Interestingly, most writers that have a pretty defined niche for most of their work usually have a few totally out-in-left-field topics. Most of my work is in B2B tech with a small portion in finance. But I also write about mental health issues. A technology writer friend writes about bowling for one client and roller coasters for another. I think that almost all writers fall in the big gray area between generalist and niche writer. And that's a great thing.

However, content marketing clients want writers that know their industry and topics. If you approach potential clients completely as a generalist and explain that you can write about any topic, then you are likely to have a hard time landing gigs. Generalists just need to be a little bit more strategic about their marketing.

The trick is that when you approach clients, you need to present yourself as if their topic is your main niche. I am not in any way suggesting overstating your expertise or pretending to be something you are not. I'm talking about packaging up the experience you do have in a way that helps the client immediately see how you can help. You can do this and still have the freedom to write about any topic that you want. I will explain exactly how to do this when contacting potential clients in chapter 5. The only real tricky part of being a true generalist in content marketing is deciding how to market yourself on your website and LinkedIn profile, which I will talk about more in chapter 7.

Identifying Your Niches

It's a fact that certain niches, such as technology, finance and specialized health fields, tend to pay better. As a result, many writers, especially those in the more saturated fields like parenting, travel and food, often want to move into those niches to get a higher paycheck. And this is a good move, assuming you are interested in these fields, or you can find a specialized niche within one of the topics that you care about. But it often falls flat and goes nowhere if your only motivation is money. It's important to pick a niche that you are interested in.

I help a lot of writers move into different niches or find more work in their own niches. And most of those writers end up meeting their goals. But over the years, there have been a few times I haven't been able to figure out why they never took off in these new niches, because I knew firsthand that there was work. It hit me that the reason is most likely that they did it because they thought they should, not because they wanted to.

Many writers panic about having to figure out their niches. But the answer is almost always already there, sitting in the clips, a past job or even a hobby. However, it's important to identify the best niches for a freelancer career and to make sure you aren't unnecessarily limiting yourself. Here are three ways to identify your niches:

Method #1: Find Niches in Your Clips
The easiest place to find niches is in your clips. If you have written parenting articles, you can use any clips you have on nutrition or exercise to market yourself to brands selling healthy foods. Or if you have written on travel, consider contacting brands that organize tours to destinations you have written about and pitch the idea to write a travel blog for their website with travel tips to those destinations.

• **Look at all of your current clips and create a list of topics.** Go through all of your writing clips and create a list of the general topics you have written about. Be sure to go through older clips and those no longer available online. Make a list of all the topics that you have written about and keep track of how many times you have covered the subject. Look deeper than just parenting or travel, and list specific topics within general categories. Maybe you have written multiple articles on mealtimes with children.

Or perhaps you are a personal finance writer but have a number of clips on saving money while on vacation.

• **Determine topics you have written about multiple times.** Once you have a list of topics you have written about, look through the list and determine what areas you have at least three to five clips in, preferably more. Be sure to consider secondary subjects within articles as well. For example, I recently wrote a story for a hospitality technology client about optimizing websites, and one of the topics I discussed was responsive design, which is a new trend in websites. So I would put this article in the categories of technology, web design, hospitality and responsive design.

Method #2: Consider Previous Jobs
I wanted to get some financial writing clients a few years ago but didn't have any financial clips. I sent out email after email, but kept hearing crickets. Then one day I was updating my resume and I realized that I actually had financial writing experience, but it was in the form of a full-time job as a technical writer for a well-known accounting firm. I felt like an idiot. I quickly revamped my Letter of Introduction to highlight my experience writing about financial topics for four years at a full-time job and quickly began receiving assignments for financial writing.

• **Pull out your resume.** Look carefully at each job and consider what experience you learned that could be translated into a niche. Did you work as a customer support representative at a software company? Maybe you were a paralegal for 10 years before going to journalism school? Or perhaps you owned a business or worked as a manager at a fast food restaurant? All of these experiences gave you knowledge you can translate into a niche and use to land content marketing writing jobs.

- **Think about the jobs that you didn't put on your resume.** Did you work part-time in an insurance office during college? Or worked retail throughout high school and college? Although these jobs may not hold as much weight with potential clients as a professional position might, they can still be used to position your expertise.

Method #3: Think about Your Hobbies

Writers often forget about their hobbies and interests when brainstorming niches and marketing ideas. However, I have found pastimes are a creative source of niches. I often ask writers who are struggling to find niches related to what they like to do in their spare time. Without fail, their faces light up and their notepads are quickly filled with marketable ideas.

I also recommend hobbies as a source for niches for journalists who are concerned about conflict of interest, because hobbies are often different than the topics they write about for publications.

- **Make a list of all of your hobbies.** Think about any topic that you have significant expertise and interest in. Don't limit yourself to current hobbies but include your past hobbies as well. Look through your bookshelves at home to find topics you regularly read about to help spark your memory. In addition to hobbies, such as golf or photography, a niche can be a topic that you have significant interest in, such as World War II or organic gardening.

- **Think about yourself as the audience.** For most hobby related niches, you are perfect for gigs because you are actually a member of the target audience. A soccer player picked that niche because she was in her 40s and loved to play soccer on the weekend in a league. In addition to her passion and experience, she was also the target market for the companies she was pitching. She understood firsthand the problems that women soccer players have as well as knew exactly what products both she and her teammates purchased for their hobby.

Breaking Into a New Niche

So how do you break into a new niche if you don't have clips or experience? I get this question all of the time and I faced this exact same issue when I first started out. The secret is to be very strategic in choosing the topics you write about. Decide what niche you want to move into and then figure out how you can use the clips and gigs you already have to move into the niche you want. For several years while I was moving up, I tried to make sure I could use as many clips as possible to grow my business, either because the clip was prestigious or the topic was one I could use to get other gigs.

Using the Bridge to a New Niche Trick

The secret is using the Bridge to a New Niche Trick. A few years ago, I wanted to get into hospitality writing, but I had no clips. I had many clips in small-business writing, tech clips and feature stories galore. But every time I approached a hospitality content marketing client, they wanted hospitality clips.

Then one day, I was pitching my weekly stories to a well-known journalism small-business website where I was a regular writer, and I got the idea to pitch some stories for small-business owners in the hospitality industry. The idea was that those stories would give me the needed hospitality clips. It worked. The editor loved my idea for a profile on a green hotel and gave it the green light (pun intended). A few weeks later, I wrote a story about managing teen employees and used restaurant and hotel sources as my examples. Not that long after, I pitched another article about using iPads in the hospitality industry. I kept intermixing a few hospitality stories with my other topics for the next few months until I had several solid hospitality clips.

I then took my clips and pitched to a hospitality technology magazine that was a perfect blend of my tech niche and my budding hospitality niche. They didn't need as many hospitality clips, since I also had specialized knowledge from the tech side. I ended up writing for this pub for many years as a contributing editor and have branched into many more hospitality markets, including landing a regular gig with Samsung. Those four stories helped launch me into a new niche—hospitality technology—that has been very profitable because there are not busloads of hospitality tech writers.

And so was born one of my favorite and most successful strategies for growing my business—purposely pitching double-niche stories, which I define as stories that cross multiple niches. A writer friend who wrote about tennis regularly for several publications told me a few years ago that she wanted to get into personal finance writing but didn't have the clips. I suggested the Bridge to a New Niche Trick to her and brainstormed a number of stories that she could pitch to her tennis clients and also use as personal finance clips—how to budget for tennis tournaments, the best rewards credit cards for tennis players, retirement saving for tennis professionals, and how to decide whether joining a tennis club was a smart financial move.

If you are new to freelance writing, you can use this trick also. Start with a niche where you already have clips (maybe from a past job) or expertise (from a hobby, life experience or past job) and get work in that niche. You can get clips and money and most importantly, momentum in freelance writing. Then using the work that you get in that niche, figure out what niches you really want to write in and use my Bridge to a New

Niche Trick to move from your current starter niche to where you really want to be. Here are three important things to keep in mind with double-niche stories:

• **The story must be completely relevant and interesting to your current client and audience.** If you pitch stories that are not a match for what your current editor wants, then you may soon find yourself down a client. This is the most important priority when pitching a double-niche story.

• **Think of writing double-niche stories as a long-term strategy, not a quick fix.** In fact, whenever possible, especially when you are growing your business, you should be thinking about how you can use each story that you write to gain future business.

• **Intermix the stories about your new niche with other stories that you pitch.** I waited a few weeks between hospitality stories and wrote about many other topics. This way, I wasn't short-changing my current client or readers.

There are five steps to pitching double-niche stories when using the Bridge to a New Niche Trick:

1. Make a list of three to five new niches that you want to branch into.
The niches should be in demand, not oversaturated with writers and very specific. Typically, the more expertise and experience a niche requires, the fewer writers working in that field. Also, the more specific the niche, the less demand there typically is. For example, there are a gazillion health writers, but you have much less competition if you specialize in gastrointestinal issues. Generally speaking, niches like parenting, travel and lifestyle tend to have much more competition because it takes less expertise to write on these topics.

Most important, you should enjoy writing about the topics and find them interesting. I have never been successful in a niche that I didn't find interesting but started writing about just because I thought I could earn a lot of money.

2. Make a list of the current publications you write for that have editors who ask for pitches.
These may be either journalism or content marketing clients. I will talk in-depth in chapter 4 about how to find content marketing clients and who to contact.

3. Think about the readers of your first client publication.
Go through each of the niches you listed in step 1 to see if any of those topics would be of interest to the client.

4. If yes, then brainstorm specific topics for the niche and the client.

5. Repeat steps 3 and 4 for each client and each niche listed.
Hopefully, at this point, you will have a list of story ideas that you can begin to pitch from each of the niches.

Add a B2B Technology Niche Even If You're Not a Geek

If you talk to a technology content marketing writer these days, they are likely to tell you that business is booming, not that they are just doing well. The majority of writers I know have more work than they can handle and are turning down well-paying gigs simply so they have time to do important things like sleep, eat and shower.

With technology involved in almost every part of our lives these days, there is a tremendous need for content in this area. Technology has invaded pretty much every single industry. This means a ton of content is needed in the B2B technology industry, but typically there are not enough writers. The reason is that in order to write in this space, you have to have some expertise in the subject matter. It's not something just anyone can write. The other reason is that many writers think that B2B technology sounds super boring or very intimidating or both.

I think that the majority of writers (even those who are not overly technical) can dramatically increase their income and expand their potential clients by adding a B2B technology niche. My exception is writers who really dislike technology and do not find it the least bit interesting. In this case, you are probably better off sticking to other niches. But I really think that writers with a moderate interest in technology can be very successful in this area.

For example, the hospitality technology niche is full of companies selling technology products to hotels, such as property management software systems to manage all aspects of the hotel. This can be anything from tablets so that housekeeping can work more efficiently to digital signs that change based on which guest is walking by to sensors for the room that turn off lights or adjust the temperature based on the guest preference and even open the blinds when a guest returns after being out and about. Because the audience is non-technical, you don't have to be a techie to write the content—just understand the job of the audience (running a hotel) and their challenges.

It's not just hospitality that needs B2B technology writers. There is a huge need for marketing technology writers (known as MarTech), financial technology writers (referred to as FinTech), healthcare technology writers (HealthIT is the term here) and education technology (you guessed it, EdTech). All of these areas always seem to be looking for writers and there are not a ton of writers pounding the door for these.

Trust me that you don't have to be a technology geek. You just have to understand the target industry and be interested in learning how technology is used to run that business. Odds are you already know more than you think you do. And with just a little bit more knowledge, you can significantly expand your client list.

⊘ **Build Your Business:** Do a Google search on each of your niches plus the word "technology." This will give you ideas of the type of gigs you can get by adding a tech angle to your niche. Make a plan for how you can get any additional clips you need to move into this niche, such as using the Bridge to a New Niche Trick.

KEY TAKEAWAYS:
Niches – Find Your Area of Expertise

- Niches make it easier to identify and land clients.

- You can have as many niches as you want.

- Look for niches in your past clips, previous jobs and hobbies.

- Consider adding both a B2B and a technology angle to your niches.

- Use the Bridge to a New Niche Trick by pitching double-niche stories to get clips that will move you into a new niche.

Chapter 4

Find Your Perfect Clients

The most common question I get about content marketing is "How do I actually find clients?" I find that almost all writers get stuck on this point, regardless of whether you have been a successful journalist for 30 years and are adding content marketing writing or are launching a brand-new freelance career. The reason is that, unlike consumer and trade pubs, there is no set list you can Google or browse for on the newsstand. I recommend you start by realizing that there is no magic list to search for nor any road maps to follow. You have to use your creativity and research skills to find the right clients for you.

In this chapter, I'm going to give you the nuts and bolts on how and where to find potential clients. But before we get into the specifics, it's important to take a minute to think about your perfect client. There is no one perfect client for every writer, but there are perfect clients out there for you.

The Perfect Client for You

I recently got hired for a project that seemed like a perfect fit for me—writing case studies for a tech firm. But within a week, it was obvious that I was completely the wrong writer for the project. They wanted very concise copy with about 20 different details located in different documents. As you can tell, I am more of a rambling writer and details are not my forte. This meant I was earning a lower hourly rate because of revisions. Not to mention I was very stressed because it took so much energy to do tasks that were out of my wheelhouse.

After two days of staying up till midnight trying (and failing) to deliver what the client wanted, I told the client I was not a good fit for the project. He very quickly agreed and took me off the project. On the surface it had seemed like the perfect project until I started working on the case studies. I was bummed that it didn't work but relived. A writer friend of mine also worked on the project and had no issues. It doesn't mean that he was a better writer than me, just that he was a better fit for this specific client.

This is the thing: there is no perfect client. There is just a perfect client for you. The trick is finding the clients from the millions of possibilities who are the perfect clients for your skills, expertise, strengths and personalities. And yes, that is as hard as it sounds.

A quick caveat to all of this: there are some things that make a client a crappy client for any writer, such as not paying, paying late and indemnification clauses. It's important to share these things with other writers and check in with other writers who have worked for a client you are considering. And of course, any client that asks you to do anything unethical should get an automatic trip to Dante's Circles of Hell.

It's easy to focus on the type of clients you enjoy, which is an important part of the equation. It's even more important to realize which types of clients you are most successful working with and turn them into long-term clients. That is really where you grow your business and your income because you spend less time marketing. The secret is identifying your unique strengths and matching them up with what the client finds most important.

I am great with coming up with ideas, conducting interviews with technical people and writing articles that translate geeky stuff into 'real people' language. Clients that value these skills give me repeat work and tell me I am one of their favorite free-lancers. And they see the trade-off of giving my stuff an extra glance despite my dropped words, because the other skills and value I bring to the table make it worthwhile.

On the other hand, clients who are extremely detail oriented find my occasional typos annoying. I am the typo queen, and no matter how hard I try (including hiring a proofreader), a dropped word or typo will usually sneak through. This is especially true with clients who assign all the stories, because I am not making their job easier with my abundance of topic ideas. Those who aren't looking for geek-to-business translation don't turn into long-term clients because I blend in with the other writers on other assignments.

One of the best clues to which clients you will be successful with is to look at your long-term clients. For example, if you have two universities that are very happy clients, then consider looking for other universities. If you find that most of your long-term clients are medium-sized businesses that write mainly blogs and whitepapers in a conversational tone and tend to work very far out in advance, then look for more of that type of client. If you have had four failed attempts with different startups, which has happened to me, then that probably isn't your ideal client.

As you grow your business, think about what type of clients you would like to add. Do you want to add more direct clients instead of mainly agencies? Is there a niche that you think has become more profitable, but you aren't currently getting much work from? Are you looking for more local clients so you can have more face-to-face interaction or perhaps the opposite? Once you've identified the *types* of clients you'd like to add to your roster, use the information in this chapter to find *specific* companies and agencies. You can contact these companies using the information in chapter 5 on writing Letters of Introduction.

ⓘ Build Your Business: Make a list of all of your long-term clients. Write down the details of these clients. Look for similarities and then look for clients with these characteristics. Then take it a step further and make a list of clients that haven't worked out for you. Create a list of these characteristics and try to screen clients to avoid these characteristics since you are much less likely to be successful with these clients.

Should You Work with Agencies or Direct Clients?

If you ask a room full of freelance writers this question, most automatically assume direct businesses are better clients because of the belief that you make more money working with direct clients. And yes, that can be true in some cases. But in my experience, it's not the blanket statement that some writers make it out to be. I have made more money with agencies on some projects. In other cases, projects with direct clients have been more lucrative. You can have great experiences and make a high hourly rate with both types of clients, depending on the project.

Some writers dismiss agencies because they think that all are low paying. Yes, there are some agencies that pay ridiculously low rates, but there are also some agencies where you can earn $200 an hour on the right project. Some writers give up after sending a few LOIs to agencies, but the problem may be that they are marketing themselves as a generalist when the agencies want to find a writer with experience in their clients' specific industries.

Each writer has to find the balance of clients that works best for their personality, their industry and the work/life balance that they want. For me, it's a mix of both, with more clients on the agency side. For the past year or so, I've been keeping a list of the upsides of each type of client based on my own experience and stories that other writers have shared with me. Here's that list:

Benefits of Working Directly with Businesses

Note: These reasons also apply to associations, nonprofits, professionals and healthcare systems.

• **Greater ability to negotiate pay rate (and rate increases) than with an agency.** Agencies typically have set rates they use for all freelancers. While there is some room for negotiation with agencies, I have found much greater ability to negotiate pay rates when working directly with clients.

• **Feeling like part of a team.** With an agency, you are one step removed from the client. If you are lucky, you get to work directly with the client, but sometimes you never have client contact. And at bigger agencies with a lot of freelancers you may feel very much like a cog in the wheel. On the other hand, many writers who work directly with a client on long-term projects are able to find the sense of team that is often missing in our daily lives as freelancers. I love my dogs, but sometimes it's nice to have coworkers who don't want to play "throw the ball" all day.

• **Higher job security than agencies.** Businesses often change agencies, which means that if you are going through an agency then you lose the client. I have lost many clients this way. But when working directly with a business, future work is typically more dependent on your results and your work than about which agency the business uses.

• **Ability to learn a lot about the industry.** When you work directly with a business, you typically have greater access to subject matter experts on the topics you are writing about. In addition to making it easier to get information as mentioned above, I have also found that I have many more opportunities to ask questions about the subjects I am writing about and really gain a higher level of expertise in the niche.

• **More opportunity to participate in content marketing strategy.** I love being able to plan an editorial calendar, work on audience personas, plan social media strategy and be involved with tracking metrics. But agencies typically handle these tasks and freelancers are usually not involved, unless you are hired for a strategy role by an agency. When working directly for a business, it is a lot easier to get involved in working with personas, determining the best type of content to create and creating an editorial calendar.

Benefits of Working with an Agency

Working with agencies can have benefits, too.

• **Often higher hourly rates.** Agencies typically come up with the story ideas, find the sources and handle the schedule. I have even had a client pay me $1 a word and hand me an already approved outline for the project along with transcriptions of the source interviews. When the agency takes care of the details, you can focus on writing, which often results in a higher hourly rate. Agencies also typically have a project manager who handles the project management details that writers typically tend to when working directly with a business. This means that when evaluating a rate from an agency, it is very important to find out what tasks the agency handles. Sometimes what looks like a low rate is actually a high rate because the freelancer is required to do less work.

• **Access to graphic designers and editors.** As mentioned before, I am the typo queen and should never be the last set of eyes to look at a piece of content. When I work with a business, I typically hire my own editor since there is not often an editor on the project. Agencies tend to have an editor on the team, and while I do my absolute best to avoid typos, those editors are generally fine with catching the occasional error. Agencies also frequently have graphic designers who can help with charts and illustrations, while businesses have asked me to hire my own designer. Although it's totally feasible to do this and some writers go this route, I didn't want another aspect of the project to manage and be responsible for.

• **Opportunities to work on other agency projects.** When working with an agency, you are typically brought on for a specific project, but once you do a great job, most agencies are willing to put you on other projects. This is a great way to get more clients for no marketing time and also expand your niches and types of writing.

• **Ability to focus only on writing.** This is a plus or minus, depending on your perspective. Typically, with agencies I only have to worry about writing. I don't have to handle project management, strategy, social media, finding sources or all of the other million things that are involved with creating a piece of content. My job is to write fantastic content.

• **Understanding how to work with freelancers.** Most agencies have been working with freelancers for a long time and have a set of processes for working with writers, such as project tracking, submissions and invoicing. They also understand how freelance writers work. But when you work with a business, you may be the first freelancer they have ever used. I have found that this means you often have to forge your way through the process and also set boundaries much more than with agencies.

For me (and most other high-income content marketing writers I know), the answer is a mix of both agencies and direct clients. This way you can have the advantages of both. And by carefully picking the agencies and direct business clients you work with, you can often minimize the disadvantages. For example, I find agencies that handle all of the project management tasks, so I can spend less time on the project, resulting in a higher hourly rate to offset the cut that the agency takes. And when I work directly with businesses, I look for businesses that have experience with freelancers so that I have to spend less time teaching them how to work with a freelance writer.

Finding Content Marketing Agencies

Here are some ways to find content marketing agencies:

• **Do an internet search for agencies in your local area.** Search for content marketing, marketing, advertising and public relations. Even seemingly small agencies often have at least one major client. I live in a small suburb and an agency that I freelanced for—right here in my two-McDonald's town—worked with a major telecommunications company. Agencies often prefer working with local freelancers, even though you work at home not at their office.

• **Perform an internet search for agencies specializing in your niche.** Many agencies specialize in certain type of clients. While you might expect that there are agencies that specialize in broad topics, like health and technology, I have been shocked that almost every time I looked up what I thought was a very narrow niche, I found agencies that specialized in it. I have run across agencies specializing in everything from construction to educational technology to hospitality technology.

• **Ask other writers.** Since some agencies hire freelancers more than others, compare notes with other freelancers about agencies that they have worked with. Be sure to share your leads as well.

• **Check out the Content Marketing Institute (CMI) Agency Directory.** If you haven't checked out the CMI website (content-marketinginstitute.com), it's a great resource for writers. CMI is a community with information, Twitter chats, and conferences. In addition to hundreds of articles about all aspects of content marketing, CMI publishes the most impressive list of agencies I've seen, and it is an absolute gold mine for freelancers. There are over 300 agencies, and many of the listings include contact names and emails, which is a jackpot. I am sure that not all of these agencies use freelancers, but having the names will save you a lot of time searching for the right person to contact.

• **Reach out to agencies on the list of agencies published in** *Chief Content Officer* **magazine.** While there is some overlap with this list and the CMI list (CMI produces the magazine), this includes each agency's notable clients and also breaks down agencies for each niche, which is not listed in the online database. You can download a copy on the CMI website and also order a free subscription to the magazine. Note that this list is several pages long so be sure to scroll through.

• **Look at Moz's List of 50 Recommended Agencies.** While a few of the firms on the Moz list (https://moz.com/rand/recommended-list-seo-consultants) are also on the CMI list, many of them are not. This list also contains additional information about the firms, especially their niches, services and size of the agencies. One of the nice things about this list is that it is curated as recommended agencies and not just a list of all agencies, so you have a higher level of confidence that you are approaching a reputable agency.

• **Introduce yourself to the members of the Content Council with clients in your niche.** The Content Council is an organization geared to large agencies and it has a member list on its website (https://thecontentcouncil.org/Members) with contact names. In 2017, I earned at least $40K of my income solely from agencies on that list. While it is possible for writers to join the organization or attend the conference, I have heard from other writers that it is not really worth the investment. Be sure to also check out the case study section for a list of specific publications. You can often find the editor directly responsible for the publication instead of having to go through the main gatekeeper at the agency.

Tips for Getting Hired by Agencies

Here are some tips for getting hired by an agency that I've learned from helping my agency clients hire writers and from talking to agencies about hiring writers:

• **Highlight your niche.** Agencies really want to know your niche. Many writers think that they are limiting their options by proclaiming a niche, but it is actually the opposite. If you market yourself as a generalist then you will very likely not get any work. Clients want industry expertise and agency project managers want to work with people who know their stuff. It's fine to state two niches, but more than that is overwhelming.

• **Use the client list on the website to get an idea of the types of clients, but not to apply for a specific project.** More than likely the agency has all the current and ongoing projects staffed at any given time. The best way to get work is through a new project, so don't focus your introduction on a specific client project you see on the website.

• **It can take a long time to get work.** I have gotten work through an agency three years after my initial contact. It wasn't until then that a project needing my experience came up. I kept following up and the client was a great source of work for several years.

• **Follow up.** You want to be on their mind before the new project hits their desk so that they will immediately think of you. The trick with agencies is to follow up regularly and stay on their radar. As your niches and experience change, be sure to update the agencies.

(!) Build Your Business: Do a Google search of content marketing agencies in your niche. Create a list to use for sending out LOIs.

(!) Build Your Business: If you currently have any agency clients, send an email to ask if they need freelance writers on any other client projects. If you have niches that they don't know about, be sure to share your expertise.

Finding Work Directly with Businesses

Working directly with a business can be very lucrative and a great learning experience. Many writers limit themselves when brainstorming businesses by focusing on products based on their knowledge, which means that they only identify a small fraction of the potential clients for which they are qualified. The trick is that you have to start with the audience. Below is my Audience First Method for finding potential clients to approach. Do not skip over this three-step process. Spend a considerable amount of time on step 2.

Step 1: Think of an audience that you know and understand. You could be a member of this audience, or you may have written for this audience extensively, or you have an understanding of this audience from a past job (gardeners, for example). The key is that you understand the daily life of this audience and, most importantly, their challenges.

Step 2: Make a list of all of the products and services your audience needs.

What things does this audience buy regularly and who do they hire to provide services? Don't just do this in your head but write a list. I promise you will continue to add to this list once you get going. I also highly recommend finding a few people in this audience and asking them about products that they buy regularly. The trick here is to be as detailed and out of the box as possible. For example, gardeners buy plants, soil and seeds, but they buy so much more. When I was starting a garden, I bought all kinds of fancy garden tools, a padded cart to sit on, special soap to get the dirt off my hands, a wheelbarrow, a kit to start my flowers before the last frost date, food for my roses and some sonic sound thing that was supposed to keep the deer from eating my hostas (spoiler alert: it didn't work). If I were doing this for real, I would call several friends who love to garden and visit a local gardening shop to get ideas. Take your time and come up with as many ideas as you can.

Step 3: Pick one of the products/services listed and then make a list of brands producing those products and services.
I know it's tempting to start here or skip to this step, but don't do it. Only start this list once you have a very detailed and extensive list of products. And I highly recommend starting with one very specific product or service from your list, otherwise you are right back where you started with too many choices. Do a Google search and make a list of all of the companies that sell these products and services. While a gardening writer should definitely approach Home Depot, Lowe's and their local gardening stores, I am mainly talking about the companies that make these products and sell directly. This your list of potential clients. So for the gardening example, I would start with companies selling seeds and make a list of all of those companies because they need content about gardening to help gardeners find their site. But I would also look at the more obscure products like the soap and the sonic deer deterrent.

A Real-Life Example

Let's use travel as an example since I often hear travel writers say that they find it hard to find content work. I promise that you can use this technique for any niche.

Step 1: If travel is your niche, one audience you should understand is travelers. It's tempting to just start with your niche, but that is a bit too broad. So let's break it down to family travel, meaning parents traveling with kids, as an example of a narrower demographic.

Step 2: First, they need a way to get where they are going, so they need vehicles big enough for family road trips, planes or trains. Some families also take cruises or tours, so you would write down providers of family-friendly cruises and tours. Recreational vehicles (RVs) are another way many families travel.

The next thing they need is a place to stay, so family-friendly hotels and resorts should be at the top of your list. Many families also prefer renting condos to enjoy more space, so property management companies may be another thing families who travel need. It's easy to stop here, but since many families are on a budget, don't forget about campgrounds.

Now let's focus on the kids. Families traveling with kids often need to rent baby supplies at their destination, so companies that rent equipment such as strollers, high chairs and cribs should be included. Other families buy this equipment for traveling so write down companies that sell travel backpacks, inflatable mattresses for kids and any other gear specifically for traveling kids. Some parents want a night out while traveling so they might hire a local nanny service to watch their kids at the hotel or condo.

This is just the beginning, but hopefully you're getting the idea. I would also include guidebooks/apps geared towards families, toys/games that are marketed to keep kids amused on the road and companies that sell luggage for kids or families. Oh, and also list pillows and blankets for kids to use on the plane, as I'm sure that there are products specifically targeted to them. And don't forget about the Chamber of Commerce and Tourism Associations for family-friendly destinations as well.

You are probably thinking that not all of these types of companies will want travel content because they are not selling trips. But they are all selling to travelers and people who travel with kids want information about family-friendly destinations and tips for traveling with kids—all things that you as a family travel writer can provide. By thinking outside of the topic, you can find a ton of new clients who need your specific skills and expertise to build trust with their audience.

Step 3: I'll pick the kid equipment rental companies as a place to start. As a travel writer, I would start by looking for national companies that offer these services. Then I would search out regional or local companies situated in the destinations that I already specialized in. Now you have a solid list of companies that actually need your services.

(!) **Build Your Business:** Follow the above Audience First Method to brainstorm potential clients for one audience with which you are familiar. Spend considerable time on step 2 and come up with as many ideas as possible.

(!) **Build Your Business:** Think about a B2B audience that you are familiar with and repeat the Audience First Method using this audience. If you are a travel writer, you can use hotel owners. A writer specializing in joint issues might use physical therapists. Companies marketing to other businesses tend to pay more because they view the expertise as a more specialized skill.

Now that you have a list of potential companies, the next step is to approach these companies.

Tips for Getting Hired by Direct Business Clients

Here are some tips for getting hired by direct business clients:

• **Make in-person connections.** You can do this by networking and by sending an LOI. It's easy to just send LOIs, but I highly recommend finding places where these brands hang out, such as a conference or association meeting, in order to make real-life connections. I will talk a lot more about networking with clients in chapter 8.

• **Be prepared to educate businesses on working with a freelance writer.** The company may not have worked with freelancers before or even considered the idea. Be prepared to explain the value of working with a freelancer and provide some best practices on working together as well.

• **Highlight your work with their competitors and others in their industry.** Yes, I know this seems like the wrong approach. I thought so also. But I found that Hewlett Packard wanted to hire me because I worked for IBM. AT&T wanted to hire me because I worked with Verizon. They liked that I understand the topics and the industry and were less concerned with me working for a competitor than I thought. This is especially true if you no longer work with the competing company. They will likely ask you to sign a non-disclosure document, which is pretty standard.

When to Turn Down a Client

I've talked about how to find potential clients. Now I'm going to talk about when to turn down potential clients. In many ways, the secret to earning high income is knowing which clients to turn down. Each time you talk to a potential client, you should not just be trying to get the client to offer you work but evaluating whether the client is someone you actually want to work with.

When you take on a client that is not right for you, you end up spending too much time on the project, which results in a low hourly rate. Odds are that your stress level goes through the roof as well. It is simply bad news all around. The secret is that there are no perfect clients—just perfect clients for each particular freelancer. We each have different personalities, strengths, goals and niches. It's up to you to weed out the right clients from the wrong clients.

Here are eight reasons to turn down a client:

1. The hourly rate is too low.

While I do not think that hourly rate should be your only criterion when evaluating clients, it is definitely a very important consideration. Regardless of how your clients position their rates (hourly, by project or by word), determine how this measures up against your target hourly rate. If the project is lower than your target hourly rate and you can't negotiate it high enough, turn down the client. Yes, there are times when taking lower pay makes sense, but it should be a conscious decision for valid reasons, such as impending bills or a sense that the experience (or clip) from this client will help you grow your business.

2. The project is a one-off assignment.

You almost always earn less on a first project with a new client than on subsequent projects with that client. You have to learn their brand voice, their expectations and their processes. Over time, you can become quicker at completing the work, and your hourly rate effectively goes up. I find that one-off projects are rarely worth it because I end up earning less and then must market myself all over again to find new clients. By looking for clients who have long-term needs, you increase your hourly rate and reduce your marketing time.

3. The topic is not in your niche.

We like to think we can write about anything, and while that may be true with reported articles in journalism, it is not true at all in content marketing. When you stick with your niche, your hourly rate goes up, clients are more likely to hire you again and your stress level goes down.

4. Your writing style does not match the brand voice.
Clients typically have a very specific brand voice in which they want their content written. If you cannot write in this style, then you are likely to face many revisions and a dissatisfied client. This does not mean you are a bad writer; it just means that this particular brand is not a fit for you. Every time I have tried to take a client with a totally different tone from the ones I can write in, it ends up in disaster. It is much better to say no and find another client that will love your writing style.

5. Your PITA (pain in the a$$) radar goes up.
We all have different definitions of PITA clients. Some writers want only a certain number of revisions or a long lead time on assignments. Others hate being asked to do conference calls. There are no wrong answers. It's just important to know what traits are not going to be a fit for you—and to walk away from clients who don't meet those requirements.

6. The client is looking for different strengths from those you bring to the table.
I never apply to jobs that say they are looking for a detail-oriented writer who turns in perfectly clean copy. That isn't me, and it never will be. Clients who want this will not be happy with me as their writer, no matter how hard I try. Instead, I look for clients who want writers who can generate topic ideas, understand their particular audience, and translate "geek" to real people. These are my superpowers, and the clients who need them tend to love me.

7. Your personalities don't match.

You don't have to be BFFs or work only for clients who are exactly like you. But some personalities are just not a fit. For me, clients that are super direct or sarcastic typically don't turn into long-term clients. I have found that I work best for clients that are real people, honest and funny. And if a client occasionally lets a swear word fly or tells an off-color joke (which may be red flags for other writers), then we typically get along swimmingly.

8. You have a bad gut feeling about the client.

This is very similar to the previous flag, but more all-encompassing. If, for any reason, your gut says to walk away, listen to your intuition and say no. Every single time I have ignored that nagging feeling about a client, I've ended up regretting it and wishing I had said no.

KEY TAKEAWAYS:
Find Your Perfect Clients

- There is no perfect client, just the perfect client for you.

- You don't necessarily earn less money when working with agencies over direct businesses.

- To find agencies, use lists of agencies, search online for local agencies and look for agencies that specialize in your niche.

- Agencies are typically very interested in your niche because their clients typically want experts in the industry.

- To find direct clients, use the Audience First Method for finding new clients.

Chapter 5

Write Letters of Introduction That Land the Gig

Once you've identified potential clients, you have to let them know you exist. Writing LOIs is the most common way for new writers and for writers new to content marketing writing to do this. (I'll discuss other ways to land the gigs, such as networking and social media, in later chapters.)

When I first started freelancing my goal was simply to get work. Any work, from anyone that would pay me good money. But that really didn't work. I wasn't getting gigs. I was spending all of my time sending out LOIs and not getting any response. It's easy to get caught up in trying to get people to hire you. But this part is easy if you have put in the effort to identify the specific clients and types of clients that are a fit for your skills and expertise. If you are approaching the right client with the right messaging, then you will land well-paying clients quickly.

So if you skipped through chapters 3 and 4 to get to the action part—sending out emails and making contacts—stop here. Go back and spend the time to really narrow your niche and identify your perfect clients. The same is true if you have been contacting clients and getting crickets—this likely means that you haven't narrowed your niche or perfect clients enough.

The Letter of Introduction

If you are moving from journalism or corporate marketing, you are likely familiar with the concept of pitching or querying, which is sending ideas for stories to consumer or trade publications. Pitches typically include a story idea you want to write (or have published), with details such as sources, scope and maybe even a quick outline of what you want to say.

In content marketing, things work a bit differently. Brands typically generate their own ideas for content and are not looking for blog, whitepaper or article ideas from freelancers, especially brand-new freelancers. They do not want pitches or story ideas. Instead they are looking for freelancers who can join the team and regularly write content marketing that fits in the likely already established editorial calendar or content strategy.

As a content writer looking to land a new client, you should not send pitches unless specifically requested by that brand. Instead send a LOI, which sells your skills, experience and expertise to the client. And yes, a great LOI sent to the right person can easily be worth $10K in work or considerably more.

Back when I was ramping up my business in 2012 and 2013, I sent out hundreds of LOIs and got many clients this way, especially through diligently following up. Over the years, when writers have told me that they weren't able to find work, I automatically assumed that they weren't sending out enough LOIs. However, I recently made a list of where my work came from in 2016 and was surprised to realize that only two of my clients came from sending LOIs. The rest of my work came from referrals from other writers, from online sources, from American Society of Journalists & Authors (ASJA) or marketing conferences and from client referrals.

This exercise of evaluating how you landed all of your current clients (which I highly recommend) made me realize that while the LOI still has a role in finding content marketing clients, lucrative work most often comes from building connections and relationships. I do think it is essential to have a fantastic LOI, both to use when cold emailing potential clients and when following up with referrals or networking connections. However, over time I've come to realize that while an LOI is an important part of landing clients, writers who view the letter as a marketing tool, rather than the only way to find work, tend to be more successful in gaining new clients. In other words, an LOI is only part of an overall marketing plan. (Marketing plans are discussed in the next chapter.)

Here are eight situations when you should send an LOI to a potential client:

1. You are very qualified for a specific brand.
If you have a very specific niche or experience that makes you exceptionally qualified, then your LOI is likely to stand out from the crowd (making it worth your while no matter how many LOIs the company gets).

2. The brand or agency most likely gets very few LOIs.
If a brand is very niche or an agency is smaller, then its inbox is probably not full of LOIs from eager freelance writers. Your LOI will likely stand out and have a much higher success rate than to a brand that gets lots of LOIs. Costco is a brand well-known among freelancers, because they hire freelancers for their *Costco Connections* publication, and the editor gets approached by many freelancers. I am currently working for a small and well-funded startup that makes team-building tools that has never been approached cold by a freelancer. Typically, the less

well-known and more niche a business is, the less chance they are bombarded with freelancers.

3. You know that a brand or agency hires freelancers.

Not all businesses or agencies use freelancers. While it is always possible that you will be the first (and I've found this to be truer with brands than agencies), you are more likely to get a positive response if the company or agency already has the mindset and infrastructure to work with freelancers.

4. The company or agency is local.

Though it is possible these days to easily work with people across the world, many companies still prefer local freelancers, even if they are totally fine with the freelancer working remotely. This way, they can meet the freelancer in person and then have the option of in-person meetings when needed. There is a comfort level attached to hiring a local freelancer. I have had a much higher response rate from cold-calling local agencies and companies than ones with which I have no geographic connection.

5. You are going to be at a conference or event with the person in the near future.

This is a fantastic use of an LOI. This way, you can introduce yourself and maybe set up an in-person meeting with the potential client.

6. You have a mutual connection with the person.

Do you both know the same person and that person gave you permission to drop their name when you introduce yourself? Did you go to the same college or work at the same company (even if you didn't know each other)? Any of these reasons gives the LOI recipient more of a reason to pay attention to your LOI and to feel a connection with you. In cases like this, I highly recommend putting the mutual connection's name in the subject line of the LOI if at all possible, to increase the odds of your email being opened.

7. You have very little work and lots of time on your hands.
If you have some extra time and really need more work, go ahead and spend a few hours sending out LOIs. It can't hurt, and you may get some work from it. Just make sure that your LOI is marketing you as an expert in one or two niches. It is going to be almost impossible to land gigs from an LOI as a generalist.

8. You are going to follow up with your LOIs.
Even back when LOIs landed me the majority of my work, I rarely got a gig on the first contact. I almost always got work by following up. I followed up two weeks after I sent the LOIs with everyone who did not get back and then again in three months. I also added "(follow-up)" or "(second try)" to the subject line to increase the odds the LOI would be opened. If you do not think that you are going to follow up, then I recommend not spending the time to send the LOIs and using the time to hang out with your kids, play with your dog or take a nap instead.

The Five(ish) Sentence LOI

After spending way too much time thinking about this, I have decided that the goal of an LOI isn't to get a potential client to hire you, but to get them to ask you for more information and start a conversation about how you can work together. I used to send out a much longer LOI that pointed out my strengths and how I could help their organization in a very writerly way. And yes, I got results with it. But I kept hearing clients talk about how they really liked short LOIs.

The first time an agency owner told me that he thought that an LOI should be no longer than five sentences, I was adamant that it was impossible. I might have even argued back. But then I realized that I was thinking of my LOI as my entire sales pitch. That actually isn't true.

An LOI is actually an opening line, a pickup line, if you will. The goal is simply to get the conversation started and get a "first date" with the client. And if I can't do that in very close to five sentences, then I probably should change careers.

Essential Elements of an Effective LOI

Your LOI is only effective if you get a response and eventually turn that connection into paying work. Many different factors affect response rates—your experience in the niche, the quality of your LOI, when you send your LOI, and who you send the LOI to. Some of these things are truly out of your hands—you have no idea if the marketing manager got back from Hawaii last night and your email is completely buried.

However, here are three things I have found to increase response rate for content marketing LOIs:

1. Additional Information about Your Experience in the Industry

Your subject line will establish your industry experience, but that's not enough. In the body of the email, write a sentence or two emphasizing your experience and understanding of the brand's industry. In addition to relevant content marketing experience in the field, be sure to include trade and/or consumer publications you've written for along with volunteer work or jobs you have held in the industry. My experience is that brands aren't picky where you got the experience, they just want you to have a background and knowledge of their topic and audience. I worked as a technical writer at IBM and always include this information when I am writing to technology brands. If you have personal experience with the topic, such as caring for an aging parent when approaching a company placing home health care, then be sure to include it as well.

2. Description of Your Content Marketing Writing Experience
If you have previously written content marketing materials, be sure to highlight this near the top of the letter. For example, "I have over two years of content marketing experience and have worked with a variety of brands, including IBM, Adecco, LinkedIn, American Express and Intuit. I also blog regularly on content marketing writing and have written several trade publication articles educating brands on effective content marketing strategy." Be sure to include associations, such as AARP, universities and airline magazines.

3. Links to Relevant Writing Samples in the Industry
At the end of your email, include links to writing samples that are relevant to the brand or agency you are contacting. I usually send three to five clips, depending on the quality of the clips that I have. Each client's needs are very different in content marketing, and I often don't have a single writing sample that encompasses everything the client is looking for. However, I am often able to land the gig by sending multiple clips that each show one aspect of what a client is looking for.

Here are three types of samples that I make sure I include each time I send clips:

• **Content or Articles on the Same Topic or for the Same Audience as the Client's Business.** This is what most clients need to see in order to hire you. Brands want to work with content marketing writers who have experience writing about their industry and their topics. The prestige of the publication or the date of the clip is not nearly as important as showing the client that you understand the needs of their audience as well as the terminology of the industry.

• **Samples of the Same Type of Deliverable.** Let's say a client wants someone to write technology whitepapers. You have significant experience blogging for a B2B technology company and have also written several healthcare-related whitepapers. In addition to including links to your fabulous technology blogs, you should also link to at least two samples of whitepapers as well.

• **Examples of Similar Tone and Style.** If you have clips that show your subject matter expertise and your skill at writing the desired deliverable, but those clips aren't exactly in the same style or tone as the client's current content, you'll need to show them you can write in their brand voice. In this case, I usually find a writing sample that is the most similar to the client's style and I will write a note explaining why I am including it.

My Sample Letter of Introduction

Hi X,

Does your agency [or brand or association or nonprofit or university] use freelance writers?

I am a freelance technology content marketing writer specializing in artificial intelligence, cloud computing, IoT and security. My clients include IBM, Adobe, Samsung, Verizon, Hewlett Packard, Vonage and Microsoft. Additionally, I worked in the software industry as a UX designer/writer for over 10 years, including IBM.

You can see what my editors have said about me on my LinkedIn profile (include link) as well as samples of my work on my website (include link). I have also included links to a few relevant clips below.

I look forward to hearing from you and hopefully working with you in the near future.

Jennifer Goforth Gregory

I've seen some fantastic LOIs that have more personality and are more fun, but I've decided to stick with a basic and straightforward LOI as my sample. I do think a jazzier version can definitely be effective if it matches your industry and your personality. But that is a very individual thing, and I hesitate to give a sample of that because what would work in one situation would turn off a client in another. A creative LOI is most likely more effective than this one, but it really has to feel authentic to your personality so that it appeals to the type of clients that are likely to enjoy working with you.

⊘ **Build Your Business:** Look at your current LOI. Does it define your niche and your expertise in the niche? Is it close to five sentences? Make any revisions to your LOI and cut it down to as close to five sentences as you can.

⊘ **Build Your Business:** Ask a freelance friend to take a look at your LOI and make suggested changes. I have gotten some of my best feedback from other writers.

An LOI for Every Niche

Like most writers, I have several different niches and use a different LOI for each niche. I always tell writers that it's fine to have unrelated niches and your LOI for each niche will probably not even look like you are the same person. You want your LOI to describe your experience and expertise for that specific client.

The LOI that I included in this book is the base template I use for general technology clients. For other niches, I customize the second paragraph for the specific niches. I typically keep the rest of the LOI the same. Here are a few examples:

Finance

I am a freelance financial content marketing writer specializing in retirement planning, college planning, insurance, credit cards and personal finance. In addition to working at a large accounting firm for four years, my clients include Ameriprise, State Farm Mutual Funds and American Express.

Insurance

I am a freelance insurance content marketing writer specializing in life insurance, home/property, car insurance, long-term care and annuities. I have written content both for consumers and insurance agents. In addition to working part-time at an insurance agency, my clients include Allstate, State Farm, Genworth and Principal.

Hospitality Technology

I am a freelance hospitality technology content marketing writer specializing in guest room technology, booking engines, artificial intelligence, IoT and security. In addition to being a contributing editor to *Hospitality Technology* magazine for two years, my clients include the hospitality market sector at Samsung, Alcatel-Lucent Enterprise and IBM.

Stadium Technology

I am a freelance stadium technology writer specializing in beacons, wireless networks, apps and signage. I have covered the stadium infrastructure for the Carolina Panthers, Super Bowl 50 and Texas A&M University. My clients include Aruba Networks, Hewlett Packard Enterprise and IBM Mobile.

ⓘ **Build Your Business:** Pick one of your niches and rewrite your LOI based on the niche. Repeat for all of your niches. Make sure that each one includes all relevant experience that would matter to someone looking to hire a writer in that industry.

Your Subject Line Matters

People only open an email they think they want to read and you won't get work if a potential client never opens it. The subject line is the key. Don't just write something at the last minute before hitting send. Your subject line needs to be carefully thought out and encourage the potential client to read your email. If you have a subject line that does not compel the potential client, then you have zero chance of getting the work and your time spent on the LOI is wasted. Here are four things to consider:

• **Include the industry of the company in the subject line.** Many clients are looking primarily for a writer with industry experience. If you make it obvious that you meet that requirement, then they will be more likely to open your email. For example, I have used "Experienced Credit Card Content Marketing Writer" and "Experienced VoIP Content Marketing Writer" in the past.

• **Make sure your subject line doesn't look like spam or advertising.** Everyone's email inbox is overflowing with advertising and most of us simply delete many emails without even opening them. Create a subject line that looks different from these mass emails so that the editor knows it is a legitimate email message. For example, avoid using the word "Pitch'" in the subject line of the email since that is commonly used by PR reps.

• **Include the words writer and freelance.** The reason for including "Writer" is self-explanatory. But many companies are not looking for more full-time employees, so if your email makes them think you want a permanent job then they may simply move your email to the recruiting folder or delete it. You also want to make sure that they do not mistake your email for a press release or pitch from a PR person.

• **Referred by.** If another writer passed on the editor's email or another content marketing manager at the company referred you, include the name of the person who referred you. However, you should only do this if you have permission of the person who gave you the referral. Using another writer's name without their permission is a huge no-no, and will not be looked on kindly by the editor or the writer.

ⓘ **Build Your Business:** Look at your revised LOI and craft a few subject lines to use next time you contact potential clients. Ask a fellow freelance writer their opinion about the subject lines.

Sending Your LOI to the Best Contact

With consumer and trade publications, it isn't rocket science to find the right person to send your pitch. It's usually on the website. And if not, just look at the masthead. All of the editors' names and their departments are listed right there. Easy pickings. The first step is to figure out who hires freelancers with your skills. This sounds easy, but it's often challenging to find out this important nugget of information. Here are three ways to find the best person:

• **Check the company website.** Check the company website to see if there is a staff directory or contact list. Ideally, you want to find someone with the word "Content" in their title, such as Content Marketing Strategist or Content Coordinator. When pitching to a content marketing agency, look for a title such as "Director of Editorial" or something that indicates that they manage the freelance writers. If it is a small agency, then I would send it to the President or Vice President, since they most likely wear many hats. For brands, if you can't find someone who works directly with content creation, look for someone in the marketing department, such as Marketing Director or Marketing Manager. However, don't contact the marketing department at agencies since they are responsible for marketing the agency not working with clients.

• **LinkedIn.** Use the LinkedIn search for the same titles that you looked for on the company website. If you find several people, read through their job descriptions to find the person who seems like they would be the most hands-on with content creation. I have had the best luck with mid-level managers as opposed to directors and vice presidents at larger companies. For content marketing agencies, you can also search for the account manager for the brands that you feel are the best fit for your skills. For example, if you are specifically targeting the Ford brand, see if you can find a staff member who indicates that they work on the Ford account.

• **Call the company.** If you can't find a direct email through your online research, pick up the phone and call the main number for the brand. Ask who handles content marketing for the company and see if they will give you an email address. If they don't know what content marketing is, then ask for a contact in the marketing department. For content marketing agencies, ask for the email of the person who manages freelance writers. This works especially well if you are targeting a specific custom publication for a brand and need the editor for that publication.

The next step, and often the most challenging part, is finding the email address for your contact. This should be easy, but it's not. Yes, with trade and consumer publications, you can sometimes get a response sending an inquiry to a generic email address if it is something like "editor@publication.com." However, with content marketing it's not worth the effort to customize and send an LOI if you then send it to a generic email. In all of the hundreds of LOIs for content marketing writing I have sent over the past two years, I have never gotten one response from an email that I sent to a brand's generic email account.

It's essential to find a real person's email to send your LOI. Your first stop should be Hunter (hunter.io) to find emails. This tool is amazing—and it's free. You put in the contact's name and the domain name of the company's website, and Hunter gives you possible suggestions for the email address. It's almost always right. It also has a plug-in for LinkedIn so you can click a button from a person's LinkedIn profile and find a likely email address.

If it doesn't work, then try looking on the company bio pages, LinkedIn, a web search or try common email formats (such as firstinitiallastname@companyname.com or firstname.lastname@company.com). If none of these work, send a tweet to your contact asking for their email address. I have had surprisingly good luck using Twitter as a last resort.

(!) **Build Your Business:** Pull out the list of potential clients you created using the Audience First Method. Using the techniques above find the best contact and email addresses for these potential clients. Next customize an LOI for each contact and send out the LOIs.

Following Up on Your LOIs

A few years ago, I sent out a batch of LOIs to content marketing agencies and editors at custom publications. After a few weeks,

I heard back from some brands and editors but not from others. I started to tell myself that they must not be interested in me or they would have responded, but instead I forced myself to take a few minutes to follow up with each non-responding editor.

And I am so glad I did. By the end of the day, I had received a $1/word assignment from one custom publication. A few days later, I was hired by one of the content marketing companies for ongoing work, also at $1/word. If I had not taken the time to follow up, I would not have gotten either opportunity. Both editors thanked me for following up and told me that my email had gotten lost in their overflowing inbox.

Brands and agencies most likely have their content projects currently staffed with freelancers. The best way to break in with a new client is to get put on a new project. However, this typically requires being on their radar at the exact moment that they are staffing up a project. And since we don't have ESP, that is almost impossible. When you don't hear back from a potential client, it likely just means that they don't have a need right this very minute. However, when you follow up and stay on their radar, then they are more likely to think of you when a project fitting your expertise and skills ramps up.

As with many things in life, there is a fine line between following up and stalking. I have asked many editors their opinion about how often writers should follow up and it seems that the average preference is about every three to four months.

An important part of following up is remembering. You must come up with a system that works for you. Many writers use a spreadsheet to track their LOIs with the contact name, date, response and follow-up. I have also been told that a good reminder is adding a calendar event to your online calendar each time you send LOIs.

I'm almost embarrassed to admit my system, but it's actually a good example of the importance of finding a system that works for you. I used to use a spreadsheet, but that didn't work for me. I never updated it. So it was always out-of-date. And while the calendar event idea sounded perfect, I never remembered to create the events.

Then I started always using the word "Experienced" in my subject line and about once a month I would search my inbox for that word. Next I would look through all the LOIs I had sent in the last year and follow up on those. Yes, an organized system would have made more sense to most people. But the key to running your own business is really finding your own systems—as bizarre as they seem to other people—that work for you. And as crazy as it sounds, this system has worked beautifully for several years now.

(!) **Build Your Business:** Think about how you want to track your LOIs and follow-ups. Create a spreadsheet or whatever system is going to work best for you.

How to Send a Follow-Up Email

Following up can feel a bit awkward. And it's easy to feel like you are bothering the person. However, the job of editors and content marketing managers is to find writers to create their content. By following up, you are helping them do their job. As long as you are polite, professional and don't email them every other day (or even every week), then you are not bothering the editor. You are only hurting your own career by not following up. Many editors have told me that they appreciate it when writers follow up because emails often get lost or buried in their inboxes.

Here are three tips for following up:

1. Put a reminder on your calendar.
When you send out LOIs, put a note on your calendar to remind yourself to send follow-up emails in two to three weeks. Most writers know that following up is important, but it's so easy to forget to actually do it.

2. Forward your original email.
Instead of crafting a brand-new email, forward your original email and keep the same subject line. This saves you from having to craft another LOI and also reminds the editor that they didn't respond to you the first time, which increases your chances of a reply. As I mentioned earlier, I usually add (follow-up) or (second try) to the subject line.

3. Keep your email short and sweet.
Write a short note in the follow-up email to your letter, but let your original email do most of the talking.

Here is an example of a basic follow-up email when I got no response from my original:

Hi Stan,
I hadn't heard back from the email I sent a few weeks ago and wanted to follow up. I just finished a big project for Verizon and have some availability. Do you have any current freelance needs?
I look forward to hearing from you and hopefully working with you soon.
Jennifer

Here is a follow up email that I used when a potential client had responded that they were interested, but not right now.

Hi Stan,

I hope the product release you were working on last time we emailed went well. You mentioned that you wanted to develop a whitepaper after the release so I wanted to follow up. I'd love to set up a call to talk about the project when you are ready.

I look forward to hearing from you and working with you in the near future.

Jennifer

Not Just Another Email: Creative Ways to Follow Up

Sometimes the best way to follow up is not specifically asking for work but keeping your name in their mind through other contact. Here are five interesting ways to follow up with a potential client after sending an LOI:

1. Share a compliment about a great piece of content the company created.

Everyone likes to hear nice things about their work. Set a Google alert for the company to get news about awards, products and mentions in the media. If you want to work for a specific custom publication, look at each issue to find something that is exceptional. The key is your compliment must be genuine. Find the great work the company or editor has done recently and write an email complimenting their work.

2. Send a link to an article that is relevant to the client.

Next time you see an interesting article about the client's industry, jot a quick email and paste the link. Make sure that the article is both helpful and relevant. By picking good articles, you are illustrating that you understand their needs and that you keep up to speed on the developments in the industry.

3. Comment on the client's social media or blog post with a thoughtful and relevant comment.

People love to get comments on their articles and blog posts. By posting on a company's blog with a thoughtful comment that illustrates your industry knowledge, you are keeping your name at the top of their mind. However, if you comment on every post or Like every Facebook post, it becomes less effective.

4. Follow up a client's recent vacation, trade show or other event they mentioned.

I landed my highest paying (and most prestigious) client by asking about his vacation. In one of our initial emails, he mentioned he was going on vacation to a place on my bucket list. When he returned, I asked him about his trip and this turned into a month-long email chain about travel destinations. People are more likely to hire you if they feel like they have some sort of relationship with you so any connection you can find is helpful.

5. Tell the client about something you have done since you sent the original LOI.

If you have written an article recently for a national publication in the industry or you have gained additional experience in the niche by working with another brand, let the client know. In this case, I typically forward my original LOI so the client has the detailed version of my experience in front of him and write a short email with my new experience and links. By doing this, you remind the client about yourself and give the client additional reasons to call you for the next project.

(!) **Build Your Business:** Search your sent email folder for all LOIs you have sent in the past six months and follow up with the editor or content manager.

KEY TAKEAWAYS:
Write Letters of Introduction That Land the Gig

- Letters of Introduction (LOIs) sell yourself, compared to a pitch that sells a specific story idea.

- Think of an LOI as a pickup line, not the entire conversation.

- Customize your LOI for each potential client.

- Do not send an LOI to a generic email. You will likely never hear back.

- If you do not follow up on LOIs, you are leaving money on the table.

Chapter 6

Create a Marketing Plan

I couldn't wait for 2016 to get rolling. I had just broken six figures for the first time and to make it even better, I already had three anchor clients (these are clients that provide you with regular ongoing work; I talk much more about anchor clients in chapter 12) plus several other projects lined up for the New Year. Then the first three weeks of 2016 happened. In quick succession, two of the projects got delayed indefinitely (both due to reorganizations at the company) and my third client decided that due to financial difficulties, they wanted 75 percent less content.

After panicking for a few minutes (okay, a day, maybe a few days), I decided to look at my empty calendar as an opportunity to see how fast I could ramp up. The first thing I did was create a marketing plan for the next two months. I committed to doing at least five marketing activities from the list each day. And most importantly, I stuck to it and hit my goal every single day, and I even did up to 10 marketing activities on some days. After six weeks, I had done the following marketing activities:

- Sent out 53 LOIs to content marketing agencies I had previously not contacted

- Sent out five LOIs to trade publications
- Connected with agencies and content marketing managers on Twitter
- Followed up on 15 LOIs from the previous year
- Checked in with five previous clients to see if they had any new projects
- Checked in with a new agency client whose project got delayed to see if they had other clients that needed writers
- Replied to 15 online job ads
- Updated my LinkedIn profile with new niches
- Updated my website with new clips
- Followed up with five people I met in person in the last year
- Sent an email to three writers in my niche to see if they had any leads
- Focused on creating an active Twitter presence with the right people and topics
- Attended the High Five Conference hosted by the American Marketing Association

You'll see that while I sent out some LOIs (as described in the previous chapter), my marketing activities included a variety of other types of actions meant to bring me and my work to the attention of people who hire freelance content marketing writers.

Within that six weeks, I was hired for about $50K of work. Not surprisingly, several of the new clients I gained from that marketing blitz turned into anchor clients and I am still working with them today, making the total much higher than I originally estimated.

When I shared the list of my marketing activities with another writer, she was shocked at the amount of marketing I had done in such a short time. This is the thing: I think that this amount of effort was on the low side for a huge marketing push. If my niche were less in demand or I were writing to pay the electric bill for my family, then I would have doubled the amount of outreach.

Feast or famine is part of the freelance life to some extent. It almost always seems as though you are either swamped with work or don't have enough. It seems almost impossible to get just the right balance. While some ups and downs are inevitable, freelancers, myself included, make it worse by only focusing on marketing when we need work. When we are swamped, we tell ourselves we don't have time to market. Then when the project ends or we lose a client, we realize there are no prospects in the wings.

Why You Need a Marketing Plan

The secret to evening out the ups and downs is creating a marketing plan and sticking to it. By a marketing plan, I mean a set list of tasks that you do every day, week and/or month. Each task is something that helps either position yourself as the type of freelance writer your perfect clients are looking for or make connections with potential clients. It's easy to only think about contacting potential clients as marketing, but there are many other tasks that high-income writers do as part of marketing. I'll go into detail about exactly what types of tasks you should be doing based on your goal and career stage.

The trick (and the hard part) is getting into a routine of marketing regularly and then actually doing it, even when you are swamped. Every writer, regardless of their income or number of years they have been writing, should have a marketing plan to follow. All writers are just a few client losses away from finding themselves with an empty calendar. Include only actions that you can take, not the desired outcomes, on your marketing plan.

I often hear writers say that they are going to find a new client this month. However, making a goal like this often feels overwhelming and paralyzes you because you don't know where to start. You can't control whether or not you get a new client. But you can control the actions that you take that will increase the likelihood of landing a new client. If you go to three networking events, follow up with 10 people you met last year, send 50 LOIs and follow up on 30 LOIs you sent earlier in the year, then the odds are pretty high that you will land a client.

A marketing plan is generally based on the research you've already conducted about finding your perfect clients. You've identified a target market (such as an industry niche) and determined how your skills and experience fit that niche. The next step is coming up with the tasks that you need to do to reach your goal. And most importantly, how often you are going to do those tasks. I've included a general sample marketing plan below.

Sample General Marketing Plan

This is an example of a general marketing plan that you can adapt for your own business. Be sure to substitute the specific marketing activities you have found to be most effective for your personality and your specific niches.

Yearly
- Attend at least one writers' conference
- Attend one national marketing conference
- Attend one local marketing conference

Monthly
- Review your LinkedIn profile to add new niches or clients
- Update your website with new clips and check links on older clips

- Search for new networking groups or opportunities in your niches
- Attend one local Meetup, marketing or industry meeting in your niche
- Have lunch with a contact, either another local writer, potential client or marketing professional
- Create list of 40 businesses or agencies to contact
- Reconnect with one editor or coworker that has moved positions
- Connect with another writer online or through email

Weekly
- Add new contacts, such as clients, sources and other connections, to your LinkedIn and Twitter accounts
- Review job ads and apply to any for which you are uniquely qualified
- Find contact person and email for LOIs to send next week
- Follow up on LOIs previously sent
- Read and reply to online writers' forums or blogs

Daily
- Send out two LOIs to either agencies or directly to businesses

The beauty of a marketing plan is that you can increase or decrease the activities based on how much you want to earn, how many hours you want to work and if you need more work quickly for financial reasons. The sample plan is one that I would use if I were starting my business; ramping up after extended time off for maternity leave, sabbatical or other reasons; or if I was in a serious dry spell. I also suggest creating your own version of this plan if you are at the end of a project, suspect you are about to lose an anchor client or already have lost a client.

Since this is a higher level of marketing activity, I recommend setting a time limit to keep yourself motivated—it's hard to imagine doing this amount of work forever. I suggest committing to this level of activity for three months and then you can scale back as the work starts to roll in. The time it will take to get the clients you are looking for depends on your niche, experience and current marketing condition.

The actual marketing activities you perform each day will depend on your specific circumstance. If you have been freelancing for a few years, I recommend starting by contacting current and former clients to ask for more work. This is by far the fastest way to get new work. For specific ideas on ways to identify specific potential clients that are likely to hire you, check out chapter 4 on How to Find Your Perfect Client.

However, if you do this level of effort for three months and do not get results, then you need to revise your approach instead of powering on with more of the same. The problem is likely one of three things:

1. You have not done enough outreach.
Most writers give up too soon. I can't tell you the number of writers who have told me that they have sent out a lot of LOIs and gotten no response. When I ask how many is a lot, they usually say 20 or 30. This is nowhere near a lot at all. In fact, I personally think that this is very few. There are two benchmarks where I recommend evaluating your efforts. At 50 LOIs, you should have gotten some responses from editors, such as "Thanks, we will keep your information on file" or "What are your rates?" And at 100 LOIs, you should have landed a gig. If you have not reached these milestones then keep going.

2. You are not contacting the right clients.
If you get to the benchmarks of 50 without response or 100

without a gig, then you need to pause to reevaluate. One common reason is that you are not contacting clients who need your experience and expertise. Go back and reread chapters 3 and 4 to try to refine your target clients. If possible, try to brainstorm with another client or in an online writer forum to get some ideas and other perspectives.

3. Your LOI is not resonating with your potential clients.
The other possibility is that your LOI isn't selling yourself well enough. You may have the experience that the clients want, but you aren't communicating yourself effectively. You might not be putting in enough details about your experience in the niche or you might be including the wrong clips. Maybe your LOI is too long or not written well enough. Ask a few writer friends to look at your LOI as a favor and then revise your LOI.

Here are five tips to help you market consistently throughout the year:

1. Write it down and track your progress.
There is something more official about having it written down. After that, use whatever system works for you to track your progress. I create a Word doc for the week and then delete the tasks as they are done. Other writers use an Excel sheet or the To-Do function in Outlook. There are also tons of task management apps available, such as Asana and Trello.

2. Build in rewards.
I love to get takeout from my favorite grill on Fridays so I have started only allowing myself to call and place my order if I have met my marketing goal for the week. For me, having a set number written down really increases my odds of meeting it. And I have to say that the reward of eating my favorite hamburger doesn't hurt either.

3. Look for markets while watching television or waiting in line.
If I am watching mindless television or waiting in the carpool line at my kids' school, I will often pull out my smart phone or tablet and search for new markets at the same time. Then, I copy the information into Evernote so I can easily access it later. Sometimes I will do Google searches and other times I check job boards as well.

4. Do marketing activities during your low productivity days of the week and times of the day.
I am slow on Mondays. It usually seems that I am waiting to hear back from sources or trying to figure out my direction for a story. So I will often try to kick off my week on the right foot with a marketing blast. I have also found that my most productive writing times during the day are typically early in the morning or after lunch. I will often take a few minutes late morning (when I find myself opening Facebook as a distraction) to send out some emails. Taking advantage of the time that I used to waste has been a huge key for me.

5. Hire a virtual assistant.
This isn't possible for everyone, but if you are in the position to do it, it can be a huge help. Marketing is a great use for a virtual assistant (VA). A VA is a person you can hire for either an hourly rate or retainer to do tasks ranging from emails, social media, editing, research or pretty much any administrative task on your plate. For marketing, you could use a VA to find names and contact information as well as send out your LOI to target markets. If you use the VA for sending out the emails, be sure that you still customize each email. I prefer to use a VA for the research and actually send out my own emails, but I know writers who have used a VA for both.

(!) **Build Your Business:** Draft a marketing plan that addresses your needs, goals and time constraints. Your efforts will be much more successful if you customize it to your own situation.

KEY TAKEAWAYS:
Create a Marketing Plan

• Keep marketing, even if you are swamped with work.

• Create a marketing plan to help you focus on your tasks and keep moving forward.

• If you are not getting a response, you have not done enough outreach, are approaching the wrong clients or your LOI is not resonating with clients.

Chapter 7

Help Your Perfect Clients Find You

About twice a week, I get an email from a potential client who found me online and wants to talk to me about a freelancing gig. Yes, you read that right. Because so many clients contact me instead of me having to seek them out, I do not have to look for work—it comes to me. I can pick and choose what looks interesting and profitable. I then refer the other gigs (many of which are high paying) to other writers who I think are a good fit. The reason I get so many inquiries is because I am very easy to find online and my marketing materials are very specific about my niches. Another reason I get so many cold inquires is that I have niches that are not saturated with writers.

The true measure of success as a freelance content marketing writer is not reaching a certain income, but instead getting to the point where you no longer have to look for work because you get enough work through referrals from past clients and other writers as well as cold inquiries from potential clients.

This is a big change from the journalism world. In journalism, you typically approach potential clients with ideas for stories. While it sometimes happens the other way, it is not very common. Many journalists have not optimized their marketing materials for being found and skip over working on their passive marketing materials. However, since content marketing clients often come looking for writers, I highly recommend focusing on this effort.

The way it works with content marketing agencies or direct businesses is that they have a need that they are unable to fill in-house or with current freelancers. Often, they will first ask their current freelancers if they know anyone, which is why networking with other writers is essential (more on that in the next chapter). Some clients also check out industry publications or similar websites to find writers. Then they will use a combination of Googling for writer websites and searching LinkedIn and Twitter to find their perfect writer. Let's talk about how to use each one to help yourself get found by your next favorite client.

Your LinkedIn Profile

My LinkedIn profile is worth at least $100,000 to me. Yes, I've gotten at least that much and probably more work over the last few years from potential clients who found me on LinkedIn. A great LinkedIn profile is absolutely essential and should be your top priority. While it is important to have a website and a Twitter presence (which I will discuss in-depth shortly), your first focus should be on creating a LinkedIn profile that is easy for potential clients to find and clearly communicates why they should hire you.

If you are a generalist or have several unrelated niches, spend some time thinking about which clients are most likely to search for you on LinkedIn and then gear your profile to be found by those specific clients. A strategy that I have seen work well includes using a generic title, such as Freelance Content

Marketing Writer and then listing all of your niches in the Summary section.

Here are six key parts of a content marketing writer's LinkedIn profile:

1. A profile Headline that Reflects Your Brand
Think about how you want to introduce yourself to potential clients and craft a title that effectively describes your brand. Since your title carries the highest rank in search, be sure to include your main niches. While some writers use creative terms such as Content Producer or Content Creator, I highly recommend using a version that includes the words "freelance" and "writer" since those are the keywords potential clients are most likely to use while searching.

2. Niches are Listed Prominently
Including your niches is the most important part of a freelance content marketing writer's LinkedIn profile because many clients looking for specific expertise use the search function to find a writer. In the Summary section, include both the general niche as well as more specific niches. So if you are a health writer, be sure to include health writing in your profile, but also include areas in which you specialize, such as neurology, chemotherapy and alternative medicine.

3. Brands, Agencies and Publications You Have Done Work For
Include the brands that you have worked with, both directly and through an agency. If you have worked for top agencies, consider adding a list of those agencies on your profile as well. If you've done journalistic writing in the past, keep those publications on your profile even if they aren't examples of content marketing. They demonstrate writing ability and industry expertise. By showing you have industry expertise, content

marketing experience and a journalism background, you can greatly increase your chances for getting a gig.

4. Jobs or Volunteer Work Related to Your Niches

If you have any jobs and/or volunteer experience that relates to your niche or that increases your desirability to clients, make sure they are included on your LinkedIn profile. I worked at several jobs as a technical writer, but I include only IBM and Arthur Andersen (an accounting firm) since both of those are related to my current niches.

5. Recommendations

When editors see recommendations on your profile, especially from top brands and agencies, they get further insight into what you bring to the table. Since it is rare that a client will give an unsolicited recommendation, use the LinkedIn Recommendation Request feature to ask select clients to give you a recommendation. Every time I have done this, the client has been very happy to take a few minutes to write up a recommendation.

If you are new to freelancing, ask supervisors and coworkers from past jobs to write recommendations. While it's best if the gigs including writing, it's fine if your jobs were in other fields, especially if the job is one you are using for your niche. Recommendations that stress your ability to work in a team, solve problems and get things done on time can go far to help convince a new client to hire you since these skills are very important in freelancing.

6. How to Contact You

While sending InMail is possible, many clients have found me on LinkedIn and then contacted me through other channels. It's important to make sure that your LinkedIn site includes a link to your writer website, your Twitter account and your email address. Give potential clients as many options to contact you as possible.

(!) Build Your Business: Update your LinkedIn profile to make sure it is easily searchable by clients that would be likely to hire you.

(!) Build Your Business: Request recommendations from long-term clients.

Your Writer Website

I'm going to make a confession. I didn't have my own writer website until 2012. Yes, I started freelancing in 2008 and went four years without a website. I used my LinkedIn profile and a free online portfolio in place of a website and honestly thought it worked just fine—until I got a website and my business almost doubled the next year. I realized I had been completely wrong in thinking I was fine without a website.

However, you can't get a website up overnight. In the meantime, create a free portfolio on Contently (contently.com) to showcase your work so you can move forward. Contently is a content marketing service that brands hire to help find freelancers and manage their projects. I talk more about content services such as Contently later in this chapter. It's fine as a stopgap, but don't rely on it as a pseudo website for many years like I did. Note that it will probably take an hour or two to get everything uploaded.

One of the reasons I waited is that I didn't want to invest the money. Yet every dollar that I have invested in my website has been repaid hundreds of times over. I get a lot of business from cold emails that find me from a combination of my LinkedIn profile and my website. And even people who find me other ways almost always visit my website. Many writers put their website way down on their list of priorities because they don't see a lot of business coming through it. But they are a crucial part of your marketing and should be a top priority.

Three Reasons Content Marketing Writers Need a Website

Having a website with the right information is much more important for writers who focus on content marketing than writers who are only focused on journalism. Here is why:

• **A website creates a professional impression.** Content clients expect that any of their vendors will have a website—and you're a vendor. A consumer pub hires you to write a story based on your ideas and writing chops while a content marketing client is typically hiring you to be a long-term member of the team based on your experience, writing style and expertise—in other words, to represent the brand.

• **Content marketing clients often go looking for writers.** Editors of consumer and trade pubs almost never come looking for writers. They expect you to pitch to them. And they have an inbox full of writers from which to choose. But content marketing clients often have very specific needs for writers, especially in obscure niches, and they will head to Google or LinkedIn to find the right writer.

• **You can control the presentation of your clips.** While I have seen writers use Contently's free profile, and I did it for a while, your clips are all lumped together. Clients can search your profile, but it can be cumbersome and your expertise is not immediately obvious. If you have multiple niches, you will likely want to separate your clips by niche on your website.

(!) Build Your Business: If you do not have a website, make it a priority. Ask other writers for recommendations for a basic site or do a Google search for WordPress designers since you can often get a site based on a WordPress template for a reasonable price.

(!) Build Your Business: Spend some time looking at other freelance writers' websites. Check out websites of other writers you know, do some Google searches and look for other writers who write in your niche. Make notes of what you like about their sites and what you don't think works well.

Designing a Writer Website That Will Help Clients Find and Hire You

Here are five elements that should be on your writer website:

1. The Words "Content Marketing" in Your Title and Tag Line
Most writers have freelance writer, journalist or copywriter listed in the title of their website as well as their tag line. However, since brands want writers who have experience in content marketing, I recommend putting "Content Marketing" in your title and your tag line. This will increase your rank in search engines for content marketing as well as let potential clients immediately know that you specialize in content marketing.

2. Verbiage That Clearly Defines Your Niche
Make sure that it is very clear on your website in which niches you specialize. Some writers include their niche in their tag line, such as "Finance and Technology Content Marketing Writer," or they include a list of niches on the front page. Potential clients shouldn't have to search for your niches; it should be obvious within 30 seconds of visiting your website.

3. Brands for Which You Have Written
The main reason prospective clients contact me is because of

the high-profile brands listed on my website. If you have created content for household names, I highly recommend including logos on your site so it is very obvious that you are a professional and have worked with top brands. You should also include publications that are well-known or influential in your niche. If you are new to content marketing writing, leave this off and add brands as you get new clients.

4. A Brief Explanation of Your Focus on Content Marketing
On your About Me page, make sure that you have a paragraph describing your content marketing experience. Make sure that you illustrate your understanding of content marketing strategy as well. Be sure to include a sentence, similar to the one that should be on every writer's LOI, that illustrates what benefit you bring to potential clients. You want prospective clients to know that you understand what content marketing is and how to use it to help their brand.

5. Clips That Illustrate Your Niche
Your clips help prospective clients decide whether to hire you. They want to see your writing style as well as the topics you've covered. However, if they don't find what they are looking for, they will leave and you won't get the gig. If you are a new writer, don't worry. Just put up what clips you have and focus on gaining clips that will convince clients to hire you. Remember to add new clips as soon as you can. Note that it's totally fine to include journalistic clips that are in your niche. Most clients see these as totally relevant and, in some cases, more impressive.

6. Contact Information
Clients will get to your website one of two ways—following a link you send via email or finding you from a search while looking for a writer. If they find you while searching, they need to know how to get ahold of you to talk about work. Be sure to include

your email information on your web page. I personally have both my email information and a contact form on my website so that clients can get ahold of me any way they want. You want it to be as easy as possible for people to know how to hire you. Don't make them work hard to give you money.

You want your website in general and your clips in specific to show potential clients you can do the job. By making everything on your site—from your clips to your recommendations to your brands to your About Me page—work to give potential clients confidence that you are a professional, your website will more than pay for itself by landing you new gigs. If you are just starting out, make your website as impressive as possible using the experience and clips that you do have. And then work hard to get and add new clips. Your website will evolve as your career grows.

🛈 **Build Your Business:** If you already have a website, look at it with fresh eyes (better yet, get someone else to look at it with fresh eyes) and make notes of things you need to change. Does it effectively showcase your experience and expertise to people likely to hire you?

🛈 **Build Your Business:** Take some time and focus on writing or rewriting an About Me page that showcases both your experience and your personality. Think of it as one of the first writing samples that potential clients will read.

Organize Your Clips by Niche

The most important thing that content marketing agencies and brands are looking for is expertise in a specific niche. You want them to quickly find clips that back up your expertise so they will hire you.

I help one of my clients look for new freelancers, and I have spent many hours looking for writers to fill their positions. I am more likely to contact a writer who clearly brands themselves as an expert in the niche I need.

If you have several niches (like I do) that are not totally related or are generalist, then I recommend separate pages for each niche if possible. It's also important to remember to change the structure of your clips as your niches evolve. I used to have the niches on one page organized by section with hyperlinks to each section at the top. This worked fine when I only had a few clips but became cumbersome as I added both clips and niches. I also heard feedback from clients that my expertise in each niche looked weaker because everything was lumped together. Now I have a separate page for each niche so when clients go to my website they can choose which niche to review, or if I am sending a link then I send the appropriate link for the client. If your niches are all related, such as health, then you can either put all clips on one page or on separate pages by subniche. For example, a health writer might have subniche pages for wellness, cardiology, nutrition and oncology.

Which Niches to Showcase

When deciding which niches to represent and how to structure your portfolio pages, think about the type of clients that are most likely to hire you. What are they looking for? Structure your clips to present yourself as a top expert with those skills and in those areas of expertise. Be sure to use the wording for search terms, also called Search Engine Optimization (SEO), that your industry uses. For example, healthcare technology is often called HealthIT so I use this terminology on my website.

It's also important to continually reevaluate the niches you are showcasing to make sure that you are appealing to the clients who are most likely to hire you. Over the past two years, I began writing in the verticals Hospitality Technology and Healthcare Technology, which are very in demand these days. I recently added new pages to showcase these specialties, and since doing that have noticed a significant increase in cold calls from clients in these industries.

Putting Your Best Clips Forward

Here are six tips for organizing clips on your portfolio page:

1. Put your highest profile and most impressive clips at the top of the list.

Many people only glance at the top of the page. Make it count.

2. Decide what to do about separating marketing and journalism clips.

If you are primarily focusing on content marketing or even doing a 50/50 split, then organize your clips by niche. Don't separate content marketing from journalism clips as this dilutes your experience. However, if you are primarily writing journalism stories while you just dabble in content marketing and you do not plan to increase your content work, then keep them separate. This is because the majority of the people looking at your site are looking for journalism clips.

Copywriting, which is marketing brochures, ad copy and website landing pages, is a specialized skill set and should be separate. It goes back to thinking about the people visiting your website and understanding what information they need to hire you, then making it as easy as possible to find it.

3. Think about what your ideal prospective clients are looking for.

Use your portfolio to showcase the type of clips that would be of interest to the majority of people looking at your website.

Are they looking for storytelling? Or technical expertise? Or is writing infographic copy your sweet spot? Put up the clips that will help them hire you.

4. Leave off the dates if the clips are old.
It's fine to have no dates. Just don't draw attention to the age of the clips and no one will likely notice.

5. Make changes to the order based on page views.
Oddly enough, a post I wrote for an Intuit blog on a portable toilet business is my most clicked-on clip. When a client tells me they contacted me because they liked my clips, I always ask what clip made them reach out and the majority of clients mention this off-the-wall clip. So I placed it higher in the order of my clips based on this insight.

6. If your clips are for high-profile brands, be sure to include the brand name on the clip.
Sometimes writers just put the title of the pub or blog for content marketing, but often it's the brand that is most meaningful.

⊕ **Build Your Business:** Is your website up-to-date with your clips? Do you have clips to add? Do all the links from old clips still work? Take 15 minutes to check your clips and add any new clips.

⊕ **Build Your Business:** If you already have a website, look at your portfolio and decide if your clips are organized in a way that makes it easy for potential clients to get the information they need to hire you. Consider reorganizing or highlighting your niches, if it makes sense.

(!) **Build Your Business:** If you are creating a website, decide how you want to organize your clips on your site. Take some time to go through them and determine the best ones to put on your website.

Should You Put Rate Information on Your Website?

You may notice that my advice above did not include content marketing rates. If you look at my website (jennifergregory-writer.com), you won't see my rates listed anywhere. The main reason is that one rate doesn't fit all situations. When rates are listed, I usually see a 700-word article priced around $400. While that can be a good rate on the right project, it most likely will yield you a very low hourly rate if the client wants seven interviews and the topic is highly technical. The rate that is appropriate for a project is really very specific to each deliverable and client.

While I aim to earn at least $100 per hour, there are definitely times where I will take a slightly lower rate, such as for ongoing work or a large volume of work, or when I don't have a lot on the calendar and I need some work quickly. When I was just starting out, I sometimes took projects that were lower in pay to gain experience or give me a clip with a high-profile publication. Notice I didn't say you should work for free or take a very low payer—just a slightly lower rate. But if you have your rates on your website, a client who may meet the above criteria and help further your career may never contact you.

Another big danger of putting your rates on your website is that you may underprice yourself. If a client has a bigger budget and pays other writers higher than your rate, but sees your low prices, then they will more than likely give you what you asked for and not the higher rate. Putting your rates on your website is akin to being the first one to show your cards.

Increasing the SEO for Your Writer Website

When I started my blog back in early 2013, I decided to pick the title The Content Marketing Writer because I thought it would help my website SEO. And was I ever right. I now have the #1 ranking in Google for the terms "content marketing writer," "freelance content marketing writer," and "Raleigh freelance writer." This has been huge for my freelance career and has helped many potential clients find me. And even better, whenever a potential client asks about my SEO skills, all I have to do is ask them to Google "content marketing writer"—they are instantly impressed with my skills once they see my website at the top of the search results.

Since your goal is to help potential clients find you as easily as possible, it's important, if not essential, to pay attention to your website SEO. Without good SEO you will have significantly fewer clients contacting you for work opportunities and will have to spend MORE time proactively marketing your services. This means that you will have less time to do paying work and will earn a lower income.

SEO is a complicated topic that is continually evolving. While I have a solid understanding of SEO and have achieved great SEO for myself, I do not profess to be an expert on the overall subject and am going to focus this section specifically on a writer's website. Even more important, it is likely that any very specific advice will be out-of-date before you finish reading this page. I highly recommend checking out Rand Fishkin and Moz's articles on SEO to keep up-to-date on the latest advice and best practices.

However, I want to share a few freelance writer specific tips on SEO that I have used to increase my own SEO:

1. Think about which words a potential client would use to search and use those words/phrases on your site.
I recommend asking your current clients how they search. Whenever I get a potential client on the phone, I ask them how they found me and if they say through search, I then ask what terms they searched for.

2. Have a blog in your niche.
This doesn't make sense for all writers, but if it does for you, it can help your ranking tremendously. I find it most effective for writers with considerable subject matter expertise who don't have a lot of clips. You can establish yourself as an expert and increase your SEO by writing your own blog. The best strategy is to write about your niche and target professionals in your niche. Not only does this increase your SEO but brings potential clients to your site for information, which is the ultimate goal.

3. Include your city in your title.
While it is easily possible to work with clients located anywhere, many clients prefer using freelancers who are located in their local area so they can come in for an occasional meeting. Since your title tag has a higher weight in search engines, this will help local companies find you easier. And even if they never ask you to come in, just knowing it's possible is often a huge comfort.

4. Include your niche in your title.
Most clients are going to search for their topic when looking online. This is a little tricky and one of the few places I recommend taking a more general approach with your niche. For example, I include technology writer instead of hospitality technology writer and healthcare technology.

5. Ask clients to include a link to your website from bylined articles.

Google gives higher ranking to sites that are linked to from high traffic sites. I saw a big jump in my ranking after my editor at Entrepreneur.com added a link at my request from my author page on their site to my own website. Even with content marketing, I have found a number of brands that will include a link just by me asking. The worst they can do is say no.

6. Guest post on blogs and podcasts in your niche.

Find influencers in your niche and ask to guest post on their blog in exchange for a link back. Yes, I am saying to write for free, so this should only be used sparingly. However, the difference in doing this and writing for free for a client is that you are writing for free to increase your own brand not to line someone else's pocket book.

7. Regularly update content on your website.

Google likes sites that add new content. Updating your website regularly, even just with new clips, helps your SEO and ranking.

Ⓘ **Build Your Business:** Search Google for the terms that a potential client might use to try to find a writer and see where your website shows up in the search. Be sure to also search for a writer from the prospective of a local client. Pick two things to do this month to increase your SEO on your website.

Twitter: Learn to Use Social Media as Marketing

I used to be totally embarrassed about my Twitter account. I had some followers and would occasionally tweet links to my published stories. But beyond that, my account was pretty lame and nowhere near what was expected of someone writing about

B2B content marketing and data-driven marketing. Whenever I applied for a job, I hoped potential clients wouldn't hold my mediocre social media presence against me, but I'm sure it took me out of the running for many gigs that I never even knew about.

It wasn't that I didn't realize the importance of social media. Or that I didn't know how to use it. I had ironically written many articles on social media strategy and had a solid understanding of how to build a Twitter following. I finally realized that my problem was that I didn't know how to use Twitter in a way that felt authentic to my personality or business—mainly that I didn't know what to talk about or who I should be talking to.

When I hit a slow spell in January 2016, I decided to use the time to figure out how to become less lame on Twitter. And without too much effort, I turned it totally around in a few months. Within 12 months, I gained almost 5,000 new followers, started posting regularly and have seen tremendous benefits to my business. More importantly, I got a new client worth $3K, was selected as a Top 50 Content Marketing Influencer, and was asked to participate in a year-end roundup with content marketing experts, all because of my Twitter presence.

Since the latest best practices on Twitter change regularly and I'm not an overall expert on the topic, I highly recommend checking out Neal Schaffer's articles and blogs. Here are the six things that worked to help me stop being embarrassed about my Twitter presence:

1. I found something I enjoyed talking about.
I am not typically someone who is at a loss for words, but I just couldn't figure out what to talk about on Twitter. I didn't know if I should I talk about writing or talk about my niches, and if so, which ones? I realized that I have about five things I write about regularly. So I finally decided to talk about what I really care about: content marketing. It worked, because I can always find

something interesting to share or say about content marketing since I love the subject and am always thinking about it. It also made sense from a business perspective, because no matter what niche a potential client is in, they are most likely tasked with creating content marketing.

2. I updated my Twitter bio.

I changed my photo to a professional picture instead of the one my mom took of me at Christmas three years ago. I also updated my bio to include my niches and added a link to my website. As with LinkedIn, I personally think that having the words "freelance writer" in your profile in some fashion is really important for searchability.

3. I began following people who were my target audience.

The key for me was finding out who my audience was. A trick that helped me find my target audience was to follow people who were following influencers in the field, and when I went to a conference I followed people who were using the hashtag from the conference. Not only would they be my target audience, but they would also be interested in the content that I wanted to talk about.

4. I got into a tweeting routine and scheduled my posts.

Every morning while drinking my coffee, I went into Twitter and found three blog posts, infographics or videos that I thought were interesting and that my followers would enjoy. I usually added one of my own posts that I thought would be interesting as well. I then scheduled the posts throughout the day using Hootsuite AutoScheduler.

5. I added my own insight to tweets and retweets.

Instead of simply retweeting what other people tweeted, I began adding my own thoughts to all the retweets. Sometimes I added how I had seen this point in my own work; other times, I highlighted my favorite point. This was key. It helped my followers get to know me and see the value that I was bringing to the content marketing conversation.

6. I interacted with others.

Twitter isn't a crockpot. You can't just dump in content, schedule the tweets and forget about it. A few times a day, when I needed a mental break from writing, I headed into Twitter to respond to people who had commented on my tweets or start a conversation based on someone else's tweet. Previously, I was only using Twitter as a one-way broadcasting tool and just talked about myself, which (just like in real life) is super boring. It was when I started actually having conversations that I started to see business results from Twitter.

(!) Build Your Business: If you don't have a Twitter account, start one today. You can follow me at @ByJenGregory and I will follow you back.

(!) Build Your Business: Review your Twitter bio and make any changes needed to reflect your brand. Make sure that your niches and a link to your website are in your bio.

(!) Build Your Business: If you aren't using an auto-scheduling tool for Twitter, try one out for a week and see if it works for you.

(!) Build Your Business: Look at your Twitter profile and create a plan to create a presence that engages the people you are targeting. Come up with a plan for posting interesting and relevant information that matches your work style. Think about ways to increase your followers.

KEY TAKEAWAYS:
Help Your Perfect Clients Find You

• Companies often search for content writers in their niche. Make it easy for clients to find you.

• Make sure your LinkedIn profile includes your niches, clients and publications.

• Update your writer website to include the information that clients likely to hire you are looking for.

• Brands are often looking for writers that are active on Twitter and have a solid following.

Chapter 8

Network with Potential Clients and Writers

When I first started out, I used cold LOIs and responding to job ads as my go-to marketing methods. I thought it was working great until I saw the difference in my business once I put on grown-up clothes, got out of my house and started meeting people face-to-face. If you find networking uncomfortable or hard, you are not alone. Most writers feel the same way. But when you talk to successful content marketing writers, most of them will tell you their best clients came through networking, referrals and face-to-face meetings.

It's tempting to stay in your home office and look for all your clients online. And yes, you will land some gigs that way. In today's digital world, real-life connections stand out in our minds and make an impression. While it is possible to run a successful business from your house, I promise that you will see a big boost in income when looking for connections both online and in person.

Your Personal Connections

One of the biggest mistakes I see freelance writers make, especially those transitioning from either a full-time job at a publication or a corporate job, is overlooking the gold mine of their personal connections. People are more likely to hire someone they know rather than someone who blindly sends them an email.

When looking to start or expand your freelance writing business, I highly recommend starting with your personal contacts. Even if these people are not in the position of hiring writers, they likely can refer you to the person in their agency who hires writers. A personal recommendation from a coworker is going to help your name get to the top of the pile of freelancers.

If you previously worked in a newsroom or as a freelance reporter, many of your fellow editors and reporters are likely in new jobs in a variety of industries. Some of them are working in content marketing. This is a very valuable network and should be the first place you start. Here are three types of contacts to reach out to for work:

1. Former coworkers.
Think about coworkers who left for another company. Does their new employer need freelance writers? Since they worked closely with you, they are more likely to hire you. Also, think about coworkers from previous jobs, even ones you don't communicate with regularly. Look up their current position on LinkedIn and consider reaching out to them.

2. Previous employers.
It's very possible that companies that you used to work for (assuming you left on good terms) would be interested in hiring you on a freelance basis.

3. College friends.
Odds are high that most people you knew in college, both in your major and other majors, are now gainfully employed somewhere. By looking on LinkedIn or in your college directory, you are likely to find some great connections.

Attend Conferences and Association Meetings

A few years ago, I signed up to go to a marketing conference in Raleigh. I dressed up, got stuck in traffic and took the last parking space in the garage. And then I panicked. So of course I did the very logical next step of calling my writer friend Stephanie from the parking garage and telling her I was going home. Luckily, she had the time to talk me off the ledge, and she convinced me to actually walk into the conference.

I was full of excuses. I had work I needed to do. My son had to eat dinner at a neighbor's house, which he wasn't happy about. And I was tired; maybe I was coming down with something. But the real reason I didn't want to go in was that I didn't know a single person at the conference and was scared to death of walking into a room full of strangers.

If the mere idea of going to a conference or event to meet potential clients gives you a queasy stomach, you are not alone. Many freelance writers are introverts who find networking with strangers to be an extremely nerve-wracking prospect. But this is why going to in-person events such as industry conferences, association meetings or Meetups can be a great time investment —very few freelance writers attend these events, typically.

I'm not talking about events for writers, which I highly recommend as well, but about events where people in your industry are likely to be. Examples would be going to an American Marketing Association chapter meeting, marketing conferences and anything specific to your niche industry, such as technology, health or travel conferences. Here are my eight tips for networking at an industry event:

1. Go with a fellow writer.

I hesitated to put this one, because it can be easy to hang around with your writer friend and not meet anyone. But if you are both set on networking and don't stay joined at the hip, it can make networking much easier when you know you have someone to sit with at lunch or during the keynote. For me, I am more confident and willing to network if I know that there is at least one familiar face in the room.

2. Start a conversation about the conference.
The trick to networking is finding something in common, and everyone at the conference has exactly that in common: the conference. I have had great luck asking people at conferences about other sessions that they attended. The opening line "So, have you been to any great sessions today?" really worked for me.

3. Take advantage of food as the great equalizer.
Meals and cocktail hours are my favorite time to network. And I've found that sitting at a table with other people I don't know is a fantastic way to meet people. Two of the conferences I attend regularly have standing tables set out during snack times where three to four people will gather. I have made some great connections by asking if there is room and joining a table that looks open and friendly. If there are group dinners or networking lunches, take advantage of these because everyone else is looking to make connections as well.

4. Have an elevator speech that explains your niche.
When someone asks what you do for a living, have a few lines on the tip of your tongue that communicate that you are a freelancer and describe your niches. If you have anything that immediately shows your experience level, you can tack that on. Don't *just* say you are a freelancer, because the next question will be "What do you write about?"

My current elevator speech is "I own a freelance writing business and specialize in writing about technology. My strength is translating geek to real people. I mainly work with big brands like IBM, Verizon, Samsung and Adobe—these are my current customers." When I was first starting out, my elevator speech was "After working in the software industry for 10 years, including working at IBM, I recently started my own freelance writing business. I specialize in writing about technology." In both cases, the person immediately knows that I am a freelancer (and likely always looking for work), what my niche is, what my strength is, and that I am most likely very good at my job or I wouldn't work for top companies.

5. Don't ask for work at the conference.
It's easy to think that networking means trying to get clients. But I have found that the best strategy is to just focus on making a connection with someone at the conference on both a personal and a professional level. You want them to leave feeling like you know your stuff and are someone that would be easy to work with. Sometimes the client will bring it up by saying that they are looking for a freelancer or something like that. But you shouldn't be the first to bring it up. Instead, you should ...

6. Exchange business cards.
As the conversation is wrapping up, get your card out and hand it to your newfound friend. They will likely reciprocate, but if they don't and you really want to keep in touch, it's perfectly fine to ask if they have a card. I find it very helpful to write notes on the back of the card about what we talked about. If you are prone to losing things, which I am, then have a plan for storing the cards. For me, a zip-top plastic bag in my laptop bag works great because otherwise my cards end up in six different places and I lose half of them. Another writer I know uses an app that allows you to take pictures of the business cards and store them for later use.

7. Connect on social media as soon as possible.

I try to send a LinkedIn connection request that evening when I get to my hotel room or house. It keeps me at the top of my new contact's mind and also gives me a way to track who I met in case I still lose my cards. Yes, this has happened more than once. I once left all my cards in a hotel room when I checked out and then had the hotel mail them to me.

Tweeting about the conference is another good strategy. Consider reaching out via Twitter to people you met at the conference. This is especially effective if you share a tidbit that you learned at the conference that relates to what you talked about with the potential client.

8. Follow up with an email.

A few days later, send your contacts an email. I might send a link to an article about something we talked about or send a compliment about a project that they told me about during our conversation. My follow-up really depends on the conversation that I had with the person. I listen to my gut with the goal of building a connection that turns into work. If I take the soft sell approach and I hear back from the person, then I usually ask if their company uses freelancers.

(!) **Build Your Business:** Look online for industry Meetups, association meetings and conferences. Make a plan to attend two events in the next six months, more if possible.

Networking with Other Writers

The first time I was in a room full of other freelance writers, I gave a sigh of relief. I had finally found my tribe. There's something about talking with other writers. They understand the joys and challenges and struggles of being a freelance writer. Someone can only fully understand it if they live the life themselves. More than that, freelance writers are unique people. They have unique ways of looking at things; they are curious, interesting and know all kinds of odd things.

Most successful freelance writers have a support system of other writers. Writer friends can celebrate with you, give you a virtual hug when you had a tough day and give you advice when you are at a crossroads with your story, a client or your career. And writers always know about other jobs that either aren't a fit for them or that they don't have time for, so we often share job leads with writers that we know and respect. I have two special writing buddies who keep me sane and focused. I honestly would not be where I am without their support, advice and listening ears.

But if you work out of your house and primarily work with editors virtually, how do you meet other writers?

• **Online Forums.** The easiest place to meet other writers is in online forums. My favorites are American Society of Journalists and Authors (ASJA, asja.org), various Facebook groups dedicated to writers, and Freelance Success (freelancesuccess.com). If you are doing more content strategy type work these days, check out inbound.org as well. It may take a little bit to find the forum that fits your style and the type of writing that you do. Once you meet a writer online who seems to have a lot in common with you, send the writer an email and see if the relationship takes off from there.

• **Conferences.** I have met almost all of my best writing buddies at writers' conferences. There's really no substitute for hanging out with someone in the hallways, having a drink in the bar after the sessions, or even sharing a meal together. Plus, there is something fun about putting on grown-up clothes and going out into the world instead of writing at your kitchen table. I've found when I travel to conferences that I am able to totally focus on my writing business and that most of my best ideas for where to take my business have come while sitting in a conference session room.

I went to my first writers' conference by myself and was so self-conscious that I spent almost all of my free time memorizing the books in the bookstore. I felt a bit like an idiot. But since then I've learned that you simply have to just strike up conversations with people. "Pickup lines" that have worked well for me include: "What type of writing do you do?" "What session did you like best?" and "Is this your first time at the conference?" If the conference has any small group events, such as luncheons or dinners, be sure to sign up for those since it's often easier to connect over food. When you get home, be sure to follow up with your new friends. Otherwise it was just a good time not an ongoing relationship.

• **Local Writers.** Even if you don't know it, most likely other writers just like you live in the same area. But they are often hiding. Do a Google search for writers in your area, and drop them an email, invite them to lunch or ask them to meet for coffee. I have found that most freelance writers who work from home are very happy to meet another writer and to make a new writer friend. Check to see if your town has a local ASJA chapter, a Meetup group for freelancers, an American Marketing Association chapter or another independent freelancers group. Then invite the writers you connect with at the events to lunch or coffee.

⦸ **Build Your Business:** Apply to join ASJA as either an Associate or Professional Member at asja.org. I have met some of my best writer friends through the organization and made client connections that earned me over $120,000 over the past three years.

(!) **Build Your Business:** Invite a local writer out for coffee. Use Google or LinkedIn to find fellow freelancers. Odds are, they will be happy to have the excuse to leave the house.

Three Things Every Writer Should Do to Help Other Writers

It can sometimes feel lonely to be working as a freelance writer in your home office, at your kitchen table or wherever you work. But it doesn't have to be. There is an entire community of writers out there to cheer you on, help you when you need it and listen to you vent. One of the best ways to network with other writers is to help out another writer that you know.

We are actually not each other's competition because each of us offers different strengths and expertise. Instead, we are each other's colleagues. My perfect client is most likely not the same as your perfect client. And even in the cases where the same clients would be great for multiple writers, there is plenty of work out there for every writer. Helping each other is win-win for all.

I would not be where I am in my career without referrals, writer friends who have talked me off a ledge on a few occasions and someone to call when I'm celebrating in my kitchen over landing a new client or writing a story that I'm proud of. I don't think it's possible for a freelance writer to reach their fullest potential without the support of other writers and there is no reason that anyone needs to try.

But the writing community is definitely one of those things—you get out of it what you put into it. That means helping other writers. And I promise that if you do these things regularly, that karma (in the form of help from other writers) will come around and help you out when you need it, whether it's a job lead when the bank account looks lean or a sweet email complimenting you on a great story that happens to come on a blue day.

If you want job leads from other writers, the worst thing to do is approach a writer that you don't know and ask for their contacts. It's pretty much a no-no. Writers are simply not going to share leads and contacts with someone they don't know. We have worked for years to get these contacts and our reputation is at stake. The best way to develop relationships and eventually be on the receiving end of referrals from other writers is to do nice things for other writers.

Share job leads and referrals. A few weeks ago, a writer I only knew a little bit through a Facebook group sent me the link to a LinkedIn profile of an agency president that she thought would be a great contact for me. She was totally right. The agency was a perfect match for my skills. I had a few email exchanges with the president and expect to get work at some point in the future. And guess what—last week one of my clients was looking for more writers, and I referred the client to the nice writer who had helped me out.

One of the hardest parts of content marketing writing is finding the exact clients who need your very specific strengths and skills. But if writers keep our eyes out for each other and pass along gigs as much as possible, then we all come out ahead. The next time you run across a client who has a gig that isn't your specialty, take a minute to think if you know any writers who might be a fit. If so, connect the writer and the editor (after checking with both parties, of course) and hopefully you will have both a happy writer friend and a happy editor.

If you don't know anyone offhand, but are a member of a writing community, such as ASJA or Freelance Success, consider asking to see if anyone else is interested. If you are looking on job boards and see an ad that you think would be a fit for another writer that you know, take a few minutes to copy the link and email the writer. I cannot tell you grateful I have been over the years for the many writer friends who have shot over email links to gigs that matched my niches.

Congratulate fellow writers. My dogs think I'm crazy when I jump up and down to cheer when an editor gives me a compliment on a story I've worked my tail off (pun intended) for or I land a dream client. But it's much more fun to celebrate with someone. So if you know a writer who landed a great gig or you see a story that really moves you, drop them an email. Everyone loves compliments. A few quick words can really make someone's day and make them feel much more part of the writing community.

Mentor another writer. I am positive that somewhere during your career another writer or an editor has taken extra time to help you along. Maybe it was advice another writer gave you over coffee or perhaps a writer friend took the time to give you feedback on a pitch that you just couldn't sell. We all need mentors and not just when we are starting out. Every time you move up to a higher-profile publication or even to a different type of writing, such as content marketing, you can often benefit from someone taking the time to give you personal advice.

Yes, mentoring another writer takes time away from paying clients. Yes, it can be frustrating if the person doesn't take your advice or you don't feel you are appreciated. But if every writer committed to going out of their way to help and mentor another writer (even in a small way) twice a year, then the writing community would be much stronger for it. Every time that I mentor someone, I end up learning something myself from the experience. And if we all commit to giving to each other, then odds are that the next time you are looking for support as you take a big step up, there will be someone with an outstretched hand waiting to help you make the leap.

It's easy to get caught up in making virtual connections and using email. But there really is a huge value in getting out of your house. Commit to making at least one in-person opportunity to network each month. I promise it will be worth the time.

(!) Build Your Business: Make a goal of doing one thing each month to help another writer out. Watch how your generosity comes back to you in many unexpected ways. Once you get in the habit, try to do one thing every week for a fellow writer.

KEY TAKEAWAYS:
Network with Potential Clients and Writers

• Meeting a potential client face-to-face increases the odds of you getting the gig.

• Reach out to former coworkers, previous employers, previous clients (especially those who have moved jobs) and college friends.

• Go to events where clients likely to hire you will be— conferences, association meetings, and Meetups.

• Often the best job leads come from other writers. Join writers' groups, such as ASJA and Freelance Success, and network with local writers.

Section 3: Write Great Content

You got the gig. Congratulations! But now you actually have to write an amazing piece of content to wow your new client and provide value to their target customers. Since most clients are looking to establish a long-term relationship with a freelance writer and repeat clients are the best way to make a good income, it is exceptionally important to knock your first assignment out of the park.

First of all, relax. You already know how to write. Only a few things are unique to content marketing writing. For the most part, good writing is good writing. And great storytelling is going to be effective no matter the audience or where it is published. This section will walk you through the few things that are different about writing content marketing than other types of writing.

Chapter 9

Get Ready to Write

I was so excited about my new gig. A local agency I had been trying to break in with for a while had hired me to write blog posts for their client, an email marketing company. So I jumped right in and started writing the series of blogs. I was so proud of myself for getting the project done early and I was really happy with how the posts turned out.

A few days later I got a not-very-happy email from the agency telling me that the posts were not what they wanted and suggested we get on a call to discuss. I must admit that when I got off the phone, I was a bit embarrassed. I had made a number of assumptions about the post, including the tone, length and the audience, that ended up being wrong.

Yes, in an ideal world the client would have provided me this information without me asking. But even if they don't, it's up to me to make sure that I am perfectly clear on the expectations. And I've realized over the years that many clients don't even realize that they have specific expectations or requirements until you ask. This means the first step of a project isn't writing, but instead clarifying all of the details, understanding SEO requirements and finding the right sources.

Here are five questions to ask your new client before starting:

1. For what audience is this piece of content?
This is the most important question with content marketing writing. In order to write a piece of content that solves the customer's problems, you have to understand exactly who is going to read your article, blog or whitepaper. Have the client clearly define the target audience for you as narrowly as possible and then do your own research to learn more about the audience. If you skip this step, you will more than likely miss the mark with your content.

2. What do you hope to accomplish with it?
I've had clients call me up and tell me that they need a whitepaper. When I ask what they hope to accomplish with the it, they tell me that their boss decided that they need one because all of their competitors have a whitepaper. This is the worst reason in the world to create a content marketing asset. Each piece of content must have a clear purpose within the organization's content strategy plan and the writer needs to understand the goal in order to create content that will accomplish the mission. Do they want to increase website traffic? Are they looking to get a lot of social media shares? Are they hoping to establish expertise in a new topic related to an upcoming product? If the client doesn't have a clear goal, ask questions and encourage the client to define the goals they hope the new content asset will achieve.

3. Do you have a specific length in mind?
Make sure that you know the length so you don't turn in 2,000 words when they have space for 500. Or vice versa.

4. How many sources are you looking for? What types of sources? Are there any specific sources that I should avoid?
This is a very important question to get defined up front since many clients don't think about sources. In many cases, I have

found that the most important concern is not using sources affiliated with the competition. Or the client may want you to use specific customers or staff members as sources.

5. What tone do want me to use when writing?
While the samples that the company sends you will help you with the tone, it's important to ask the brand up front about the brand voice. It gives you more information and also shows the brand that you understand how important the tone is in content marketing.

Understanding Your Audience

In traditional journalism, it is usually self-evident who your customer is for a specific article, or the audience can be described in one sentence, such as under 30-year-old women who are very interested in fitness or IT professionals wanting to learn about the latest technological advances to further their careers. But because successful content marketing deliverables build trust with a brand by helping potential customers solve their problems, it is important that a content marketing writer have a much deeper understanding of the audience. Before you start to write, make sure you know the following:

• **What do they value?** Once you have a description of the audience, spend some time understanding what they care about. It's not good enough to just understand that parents care about the happiness, safety and health of their children. Or that small-business owners want their businesses to succeed so they can support their family and continue to employ their current staff members. You need to really "get" why they care and the degree that they are passionate. You will get the best understanding by talking (and actually listening) to real people who fit in the demographic.

• **What problems are they trying to solve?** Parents may struggle with preparing a healthy dinner when they walk in the door from work while small-business owners may struggle with finding work-life balance. During your conversations, make a list of these challenges that your client's customer faces. Successful content marketing is built upon helping people solve their problems and providing information that they need, so it is crucial that you have a firm understanding of the challenges that they face.

Be careful that you are not just focusing on the problems that the brand wants the customer to solve by using their products, but on all the challenges that the customer finds most overwhelming. Successful content marketing provides answers the customer can depend on, not just answers the company's products or services can provide.

By understanding the customer and what keeps them up at night, you can create effective content marketing materials that will cause them to turn to the brand for information that they trust.

Content Marketing Writing and SEO

I'm often asked by freelancers how much content marketing writers need to understand about SEO. The answer is—it depends. All writers need to understand the basic concepts of SEO and how to create a blog post that will perform well on social media without making it sound like you are keyword stuffing, which is forcing keywords into copy for the sole purpose of trying to increase the SEO. I also think writers should understand the role of SEO in the headline and how to craft a headline that increases SEO. The specifics of successful SEO change frequently (check Moz.com for the most current recommendations) but in general you need to think in terms of keyword searches the client's coveted audience would use to find information on the topic you're writing about.

The more involved you are in creating the content strategy, the more important it is to really understand SEO and keywords, in which case you'll need to stay on top of trends. However, writers who come in later in the process are typically given the keywords by the strategists. If this is you, you can get away with a more basic knowledge. On the other hand, freelancers can add to their value (both in terms of getting more clients and charging a higher rate) by being an SEO expert as well. It's really an individual decision as a freelancer. My opinion is that it isn't a necessity, but that keeping up-to-date on SEO helps you create better content that gives your clients better results.

Finding Sources

Sourcing is one of the main areas where content marketing is different than traditional journalism. If you are working on an article for a consumer publication, then it is a given that you will get quotes and information from people in the industry. Typically, the publication's main criteria for sources are that they are reputable and respected on the topic. But with content marketing, the sourcing can be tricky since you must make sure none of the sources compete in any way with the brand you are writing for. And most clients (if not all) won't want you to use sources affiliated at all with any other company in their industry. This can make it challenging to find the right sources. Since there is also typically some subtle messaging involved in content marketing, you want to make sure that the sources are representative of the brand's image and positioning on the topic.

Here are five ways to find sources for a content marketing deliverable:

1. Ask your client.

Your first step should be to ask your client if there are any sources that they want you to use. While this would typically be frowned upon with a consumer publication, it is actually acceptable if not expected in content marketing writing. Some clients will ask you to use their own internal experts while others might ask you to use specific customers in the deliverable. I have also had clients who requested I use specific industry experts that the company had a relationship with.

2. Contact industry associations.

Almost every industry has a professional association whose mission is to promote the profession. There is even a Pigeon Racing Association. I didn't even know that pigeons raced, but I digress. Do a web search to see which organizations exist for your topic and then email the press contact. I have found associations to be very responsive and the quality of experts to be very high. Typically, association representatives are also product neutral and respected in the field.

3. Search for academic professionals who specialize in your topic.

Professors can be fantastic sources. Look for universities that have degree programs (especially graduate programs) in the area that you are writing on and then search for specific professors with experience on your topic. The more well-known and respected the institution, the better. Some universities also have institutes or centers on specific subjects, which can be great resources as well. The only downside is if your deadline is over a college break or during the summer, you may have a hard time getting a response.

4. Look for industry experts.

You have to tread carefully here, but some industry experts can be great sources for content marketing. Look at conferences on the topic as well as other articles to see if you can find experts that are regularly relied on for their knowledge and are respected in the industry. Make sure that they do not have any current or past relationships with competitors. Be sure to disclose up front to the expert that you are working for a specific brand to make sure that they do not have any other conflicts as well. I have found that industry analysts working for large firms and book authors are often good experts.

5. Look for authors.

Authors who share the same audience as your content piece are often very happy to be a source. I usually start by searching on Amazon for the topic and the checking out the credentials of any author before contacting them. I also use the Look Inside feature on Amazon to read some of the content, if available.

KEY TAKEAWAYS:
Get Ready to Write

• Ask questions about the client's expectations before writing a single word.

• Learn as much as you can about your audience so you can write content that resonates with them.

• Make sure you know your client's keyword strategy.

• When looking for sources for content, consider industry associations, universities and book authors.

Chapter 10

Write in the Brand Voice

Why Voice Should Be a Top Priority

On paper it looked like I was a perfect fit for the gig. It was for a custom publication for a law firm. In fact, the editor gave me an assignment within an hour of getting my Letter of Introduction. But after completing two assignments for the publication, it was obvious to both me and the client that I just wasn't the right fit. I was frustrated at the lack of direction and the high number of revisions. And the client was frustrated because my drafts simply were not what he was looking for.

I felt like a failure. I declared myself a fraud and was convinced that all my previous success had been luck. And I had a moment where I decided that I should switch careers. Then a fellow writer friend reminded me that even if you are a good writer, you are not going to be a fit for every client who hires you. She helped me remember that there are many factors that go into a gig being a match between client and writer.

After looking at my versions compared to the edited versions, I figured out the problem. The editor wanted snappy and catchy writing, but that just isn't my writing style. No matter how hard

I tried to emulate the tone, I just couldn't get it, and my results sounded forced. The information was relevant to the audience. The story was structured in a logical manner. The writing was solid. But no matter how hard I tried, I simply could not write in the "voice of the brand."

If you ever have a client say that they don't like a piece or have a ton of revisions, take a step back. Could the problem be the tone? Tone or brand voice is the way in which a company talks to their customers. It's usually something that is established at a corporate level and is a part of the company's identity.

I have found that it is almost always the underlying issue when a client doesn't like a piece of content. Tone can be very hard to nail. And if you are working with people who are not professional editors, they may not be able to articulate that they don't like the tone, but just tell you that they don't like the piece.

I have seen many writers struggle when transitioning to content marketing writing because they have never had to pay attention to tone for the most part. While there may be slight differences in tone for different publications, most journalistic-style articles are written in the writer's own voice. But with content marketing writing, you must write in the client's voice. The journalists who are aware of this difference and actively address it are those seem to have the easiest time transitioning.

How to Determine What Tone a Client Wants

Before you write a single word, find out what tone the client is looking for in the piece. Here are four tips:

• **Ask the client.** As I mentioned above, I always ask the client about the tone. I usually get something like snappy, conversational or formal. It's not overly revealing and not enough information to successfully nail it, but it starts the conversation. I will also usually ask if they are looking for second or third person and try to steer the client to second person if at all possible because it creates a connection to the audience.

• **Ask for brand guidelines or a style guide.** Not all companies have a guide, but some do. I've been surprised at how many times clients have not mentioned these guidelines until I asked.

• **Have the client send you an example of tone.** Ask the client to send you a few examples of work they have produced with the tone that they are looking for. If someone says just look at the blog, explain that you would prefer a link to their favorite pieces so that you don't model it on a piece that no one likes. For brand-new projects, have the client send you a link to articles from other sites that they like. Depending on the project, sometimes a client will send me examples of projects that use the same structure they want and then other examples for the tone.

• **Get an example of what they don't want.** Sometimes seeing an example of what they don't like is even more helpful. Not all clients will send this to you, but I always find this interesting and clients are usually impressed when I ask this question.

Style Elements That Contribute to the Tone

The hard part about getting a tone right is that it isn't a single technique or element that creates a tone, but many different things that work together. This makes a tone problem difficult to identify and even harder to fix. When writing the draft or reviewing the examples, think about the following elements that help comprise the tone:

Point of view – I personally think that point of view is one of the biggest choices that determines tone. It's almost impossible for an article written in third person to feel conversational or a first-person article to be formal. I try to encourage all of my clients to use at least second person because I find it makes a huge difference in the readability as well as the connection to the audience. If you are working on B2B content, don't assume third person is the way to go. Many brands are now using second person for B2B, with some brands such as IBM even using first person for some blogs.

Sentence length – Longer sentences tend to give a more formal tone. If you are aiming for a more conversational or snappy tone, try shorter sentences when possible.

Paragraph length – The same is true with paragraphs. Shorter paragraphs tend to convey a less formal tone. I also find that varying paragraph lengths help to create a less formal tone overall.

Word choice – If you say, "Have a chat" versus "Have a conversation," these convey two totally different tones. Look throughout the sample piece to find the type of words used and keep it consistent throughout your work. I always do one edit that is totally focused on word choice for tone and almost always make adjustments based on the tone.

Marketing jargon – I hate marketing jargon. My current pet peeve is the word innovate because if you are using the word innovate (which everyone else currently is using) then you are actually not being innovative. Nothing formalizes a piece of content and removes the connection between the reader and the brand as much as jargon.

Em/en dashes – So I might be addicted to em and en dashes. I think that they can make a deliverable much more conversational and easy to read. I use them to set off text, add examples, context and maybe even something funny. If you aren't using this technique, start noticing em and en dashes when you are reading and see how you can apply them to your own work.

Sentence structure – My fifth grade English teacher would not be pleased with me. I LOVE beginning sentences with *But* and *And*. I think it makes the deliverable much more conversational and easy to read. I also think that occasionally using a short question or sentence fragment can be very effective to conveying a specific tone.

What to Do If Your Client Doesn't Like the Tone

No matter how fantastic of a writer you are. Regardless of how many years you have been freelancing. At some point you are going to get the tone wrong. It is inevitable. And it is usually with a new client. By spotting the flags early and letting the client know that it's the tone that you took that they don't like instead of simply not liking your writing, you can often still save the client relationship. I find this conversation is a lot easier when I have already talked about tone with the client during the kickoff call because it's not a new topic and they understand how important tone is.

You are not going to like my answer to this question. I personally think that the only surefire way to fix a tone is to rewrite the deliverable. Each time I have tried to just make some changes to fix a piece, it ends up sounding like I did exactly what I did. And the piece never really works. It lacks something.

The best approach is to rewrite the deliverable paragraph by paragraph. I will usually write the new paragraph directly under the old one then delete the original text when I've got the paragraph rewritten. If it's a long piece, then I will have the client review one section before I redo the entire project to make sure I am on the right track.

(!) **Build Your Business:** Take a piece of content that you've written recently (or create a topic idea if you are a new freelancer) and write a few sentences in different tones using the techniques discussed above. Try business formal, conversationally professional and snappy casual.

KEY TAKEAWAYS:
Write in the Brand Voice

• When clients do not like something you wrote, the issue is almost always the tone.

• Ask the client for a sample of the tone that they want.

• Use style elements, such as em dashes, punctuation, sentence length, point of view and word choice to match the brand voice.

Chapter 11

Managing Revisions

Yes, clients are going to have revision requests. You shouldn't take it personally. It doesn't mean that you did a bad job. You should expect a higher number of revisions with new clients as you learn their tone and expectations. I typically find, for a short blog post, one revision cycle is normal, while a longer e-book or whitepaper will have two or three.

But occasionally you get caught up in revision cycles that seem endless. For me, the majority of these endless revision cycles have come with working for an agency. One reason is that when working with an agency, you are typically removed from the end client and have very little contact. This makes it harder for you to fully understand the client's messaging and what they are looking for. Another reason is that when you are working with an agency, you ultimately have at least two clients, the agency and the end client, and often they are looking for different things in the deliverable. The agency will ask for certain revisions before passing the deliverable along to the client. Then the client will have revisions—maybe even changing back some of the things the agency requested. I have found that this dynamic also creates additional revisions.

However, writers should work to avoid multiple revision cycles whenever possible. Clients are typically less satisfied when they have to spend hours working on the revisions, which decreases your likelihood of referrals and repeat work. Extensive revisions can also significantly decrease your hourly rate on the project, which, over time, can mean the difference in a high-earning year and a low one.

I talk with every potential client about my ideas for reducing revisions before we agree to work together and have found it makes a huge difference. Bonus—the client is usually impressed about my initiative and shares the same goal of reducing revisions.

Writers can take steps to reduce the number of revision cycles:

1. Make sure that you are clear on the client's expectations and the scope of the project.
Have all parties who will be reviewing the document participate in the kickoff call. If members of the client's team are not clear about the direction, ask them to come to an agreement on the deliverable and let you know what direction they decide. Try to stay out of differences among the client team if at all possible.

2. Ask any questions that you have before you begin writing.
Don't write a single word until you are clear on the direction. If you have to schedule another call with the client for clarification, do it. The client would much rather take the time up front than receive a document that isn't what they were expecting.

3. Write a clause about revision cycles in your contract.
One way to reduce endless revision cycles is to ask for a clause in your contract stating the number of revision cycles that will be included in your fee and stating an additional charge for each additional cycle. Some writers have a set fee for additional

revisions while others specify that after one or two rounds of revisions the client will pay an hourly rate for the changes. I have found that the mere inclusion of this clause encourages clients to be more concise in their revision cycle and wrap the project up more quickly.

Note that I tell clients that I don't have a set revision limit but will write until they are thrilled. However, I tell them that if the scope changes then that is a different conversation. However, this doesn't work for many writers and they prefer a revision limit.

4. Ask the client to have everyone who will be signing off on the finished project review the outline and the first draft.
A project is less likely to require multiple revisions if everyone who has to weigh in on it does so early in the process. I bring this issue up with potential clients during the intro call by telling a humorous story about what I call the "Who is Ralph?" syndrome, which I'll tell you about later in this chapter.

5. Write an outline.
This is the single biggest tool for reducing revisions. During the first phone call, I tell my potential client that I have found projects go much smoother with fewer revisions if I first write an outline and get input before beginning to write the project. I go more in-depth into writing an outline later in this chapter, but it's one of those tricks that cannot be mentioned enough.

6. Ask the client to consolidate all feedback for you.
You haven't fully lived until you've sorted through the fun of two coworkers having an argument in the comments of a doc you are revising. And then you are left with trying to figure out whose comments win and what to do. While it can be amusing (maybe it's just me), it's best to avoid this altogether by having

one person be responsible for consolidating all of the feedback and resolving infighting. You are the freelance writer, not the peacekeeper.

7. Have everyone reviewing the document use track changes.
I used to think the worst offense was clients that turned track changes off so I had to try to figure out what they changed to make sure it was well written. Until I ran into the client who made her own track changes. She used color coding and underlines and comments inserted into the text using different fonts to make her changes. This meant that not only did it take me longer to figure out what in the heck I had to do, I also had to return all the formatting to its normal state. While it seems obvious, I now specifically ask clients to use track changes.

8. Specify a deadline for revisions.
The most annoying and time-consuming revisions are those that magically appear in your inbox months after the project is over. Yes, this has happened to me many times. And the record was *six months* later. Yes, seriously. When this happens, you must then find the time from your existing client work to fit in the changes. Not to mention that it's going to take you much longer to make the revisions because you will have to get back up to speed on the project since the details are likely long forgotten. The fix is to state in your contract that you will only be available for revisions for 30 days after the project is submitted.

Write an Outline

In sixth grade I had a teacher who loved outlines. Every single paper and assignment had to have an outline attached or she gave you a zero. I despised having to sit down and plan out what I was going to write so much that I started writing the outline

AFTER the paper was written. The bonus was that the outline had to be turned in before the paper, so I was always ahead just to avoid having to write an outline on its own.

Fast forward more years than I am going to put in print, and my opinion of outlines has changed dramatically. Whenever possible, I try to create an outline of my content marketing projects and get the client to approve the outline before I start writing. This is especially true with a new client or someone who doesn't know exactly what they want.

Since messaging, tone and sources are important in content marketing, I can reduce my stress, increase my income and improve client satisfaction by writing a detailed outline. If the client has input up front and the chance to make changes, then the number of revisions required are dramatically decreased. As a result, the project takes less time and my hourly rate increases. Plus, the client is usually happier, which often means I get more work as well.

I cannot recommend writing outlines enough. I started doing them for new clients, but now do outlines for pretty much every project, unless it is super straightforward.

Here are five tips for using outlines to increase your income and client satisfaction:

1. Ask the client if they would be willing to review an outline at the beginning of the project.
While a few of my clients have asked for an outline, most clients don't mention it. But when I bring it up, they love the idea and are happy to review it. In fact, I think that offering to do an outline increases their confidence in me instead of being irritated at an extra step. If a client balks, explain that you have found that adding an outline decreases the revisions on a project.

2. Include a description of the purpose, length, sourcing requirements and tone of the project.

At the top of the outline, I will write a few sentences describing the tone and what the client wants to accomplish with the piece of content. If the story is web based, I will also include the target keyword. By including this information, I can make sure that we are on the same page about all of the requirements as well.

3. For longer projects, create a very detailed outline.

I recently wrote a three-page outline that included most all of the points that I was going to make in a 3,000-word whitepaper. I included all main points and supporting points that I wanted to make in the story as well as supporting statistics and examples. While it took more time up front, when I sat down to write the story based on the approved outline, I cranked out the whitepaper in less time than it took me to write the outline.

4. For blog posts, create a basic bulleted outline.

I will only create an outline for a blog post if it is for a new client or a client who has had many revisions on previous blog posts. I don't go into as much detail for blog posts and will typically just submit a bullet point outline with my main points.

5. Note both web and expert sources in the article.

In journalism, editors are mainly concerned about the credentials of the source and that they are deemed an expert on the topic. In content marketing, brands want to make sure that sources have no affiliation with competitors. Companies typically want you to either use sources within their brand or neutral sources, such as trade organizations or university professors. By getting sources approved with the outline, you will save yourself the hassle of having to do another interview at the end of the project and reducing your hourly rate as well.

Avoid the "Who Is Ralph?" Syndrome

I had been working on an e-book for a huge tech company for two weeks and was just about finished. I thought we had done everything right: We had a kickoff call where I got clarification, I had the subject matter expert (SME) review the outline, and we went through three rounds of revisions. When I opened the email from my contact about the V4 (fourth round of edits) I had submitted a few days before, I was surprised that there was a document attached. We were all expecting that this was just for a rubber stamp approval at this point.

I opened the document and my eyes were blinded with track changes notes throughout the document. There were lots and lots of comments on every page, in every paragraph. When I looked to see who had all these comments at this stage, it was a name I had never heard of in all the project meetings and had not seen on the review of the outline or any previous reviews of the document. "Who the heck is Ralph?" I said loudly, to no one.

Apparently at the eleventh hour, someone had remembered that Ralph needed to approve the e-book before it could be printed. So they sent it to Ralph. And Ralph had lots of comments. We ended up extending the project two more weeks, having three more calls and two more rounds before we signed off. Luckily, yes, I got the client to give me some more money for my troubles. But, all of that extra work could easily have been avoided by getting Ralph to look at the outline and first draft.

So now, when I first talk to a client about a new project, I tell them this story (including the part about the client paying me more money) and they always laugh. I then tell them I find that projects go much smoother if every person who must sign off on the final version reviews both the outline and the first draft. They always agree (and laugh). I will then bring up the "Who is

Ralph?" Syndrome again during the outline phase to make sure the right people are reviewing the draft. By actively managing and keeping an eye out for this, you can save yourself a ton of headaches and revisions.

(!) **Build Your Business:** Decide how you are going to actively manage revisions in the future. Start talking with potential clients about reducing revisions during your initial phone call. They will be impressed at your ideas and you will hopefully have fewer revisions.

KEY TAKEAWAYS:
Managing Revisions

- Actively manage the revision process before writing a word.

- Whenever possible, write a detailed outline before writing.

- Avoid the "Who is Ralph?" Syndrome by having everyone who will sign off on the project review the outline and first draft.

Section 4: Make Tons of Money

I almost put the phrase *six figures* in the title of this book. But I didn't because everyone has different income goals. For one person, they only want to work part-time and earn $50K while having the flexibility to be there when their kids come home or help take care of aging parents. Other people want to work full-time and earn $100K or more. There is no wrong answer. It's a matter of knowing how much money is the right amount for you.

Every time money comes up on freelance writer groups or forums, someone always posts that they feel inadequate because they are not earning the same amount as other people. I hope this chapter and my frank discussion of money does not make you feel this way. I am including prices and earning information so that you know it is possible for you to earn a high income as a freelancer.

If you aren't at these earning levels, it is not because you are less of a good writer in any way than writers who are earning top dollars. Not at all. I personally feel that most writers who are willing to put in the effort and approach their business strategically can earn a high income. But each person's path to take them there is different. If you aren't at the income level you want, you just need to step back and figure out your unique path to get there.

I promise you many other writers ARE earning these rates. There is no reason that you shouldn't be one of them. Regardless of your niches and your experience, I promise that you can find the right angle and the right clients to move you up to this place. No, it isn't easy. No, it doesn't happen overnight. Yes, it takes some creativity. And a heck of a lot of hard work. But there is absolutely no reason that you can't be a high-earning writer.

Chapter 12

The Secrets behind High-Income Writers

Ever since I started freelancing, I've been curious about why one writer earns a high income while another person struggles to meet their financial goals. So I ask as many free-lancers as I can about how they run their business and pay careful attention to online discussions about earning a high income. And over the past 10 years, I thought way too much about this issue and have come to the conclusion that success typically comes down to three things:

- Anchor Clients
- Persistence
- Business-Owner Mentality

No, I did not forget to include being a great writer. In fact, I really don't think writing is that big a part of the equation. I personally think that beyond a certain threshold of skill, writing talent is actually one of the least important reasons. Yes, you have to be a good writer—okay, a really good writer. But I don't think you have to be a great writer, as in award winning, bestselling, one of the greatest that ever lived. I honestly think that the other three characteristics are much more important.

But back to what makes a high-income writer. I really think that understanding why someone who is a successful writer has achieved this level is really key to getting there yourself. By learning from other writers, I was able to make changes in my own business that I feel really made the difference in my income. I'm going to share my thoughts on these three characteristics, but I encourage you to conduct your own research experiment by observing high-income writers and asking questions. Most successful writers are happy to help others because others helped them on the way up and they are happy to pay it forward.

Anchor Clients: A Cornerstone for Earning a High Income

I have yet to find a six-figure writer who doesn't have anchor clients. These are long-term clients that provide regular work each month, usually a substantial amount. My anchor clients include two content marketing agencies and two direct businesses. I am on retainer with one of these clients for a set amount of work each month. The other three clients send me regular work throughout the month. A few years ago, one of my anchor clients was a trade publication that assigned me several stories a month. In my opinion, you should aim to have at least two anchor clients. Here are three benefits that I've found to having anchor clients:

• **Less pitching and marketing** – Because marketing is unbillable, it is almost impossible to earn a high income if you are constantly trying to land another project. While you do have to pitch with some anchor clients, it's typically just sending over a few ideas with a few sentences each instead of fully fleshed-out pitches. If you spend less time marketing, then you are going to have more time to take on paying work.

• **Higher hourly rate** – No, anchor clients don't always pay the highest rates. But each time you do a project for a new client, it almost inevitably takes longer than the tenth project you do for that client, meaning you make less per hour on the initial projects. With an anchor client, you know the client's expectations, the subject matter and the tone, which means it takes you less time and usually means fewer revisions.

• **Opportunity for new niches and writing type** – A brand-new client is not likely to hire you to write your first whitepaper. But a client you have worked with for two years may very well be interested in hiring you for a first run because they know your work and you know their company. Once you have an anchor client, think about ways to get new experience and expertise. Since breaking into a new niche is often very hard, keep a close eye on ways to do this with your existing clients. For example, an agency you currently work with might need a new writer for a new client launching a product.

🛈 **Build Your Business:** Make a list of your current anchor clients. Note how you found each one and the percentage that each makes up of your overall income. By thinking about your current anchor clients, you can get clues into other types of anchor clients that would be a fit for you.

How to Find Anchor Clients

This is the million-dollar question. It's more that clients *become* anchor clients than you *find* anchor clients. Late last year I decided that I wanted to add a new anchor client. The first two new clients I thought would fit that bill didn't turn out to do so for various reasons. But I recently took on a new client that I am pretty sure is going to be an anchor client in 2018. However, it will take me a few more months of working with them to know for certain. Finding anchor clients is more of a process than a transaction.

The key is that when you look for new clients, you should consciously look for clients that have anchor client potential. Here are three things to look for:

• **Ongoing projects** – I recently talked to a potential agency client on the phone who wanted to hire me to write a whitepaper. I told her that I am looking for long-term clients and asked about the possibility of future work. She laughed and said, "Oh, don't worry. If this works out, we have many whitepapers that we need written." She then added that she was also looking for a long-term freelancer, not someone to work on just one project. This is exactly the type of answer I am looking for when I ask about long-term work.

• **Matching strengths** – A client is only going to become an anchor client if they think you do a great job. But that means your strengths need to match up with the skills they want. During the initial call, I listen for the words "detail oriented" and if I hear this mentioned then I usually don't take the client, because as hard as I try this is never going to describe me. On the other hand, if the client mentions that they want a writer to be part of the team, help with content strategy and come up with ideas, then I know that I could very well be the writer they are looking for.

• **Personality** – A few years ago when I lost three anchor clients and was panicking, I made a list of every anchor client I had ever had and tried to find the pattern. I realized pretty quickly that if we lived in the same town that I would be personal friends with every single one of them. With an anchor client, you become part of the client's team and a good part of this depends on having a personality that mixes well with the other people on the team.

(!) Build Your Business: Make a list of all of your current clients. Could any of those clients turn into anchor clients? What can you to do increase the workload to anchor client level?

Keeping Your Baskets Balanced

You want regular clients, but you don't want all of your eggs in one basket. Clients come and go, often very quickly, and many times you lose a client through no fault of your own because the budget dries up, your contact leaves the company or the company changes direction. This stinks when it happens, but it can be disastrous when it is an anchor client.

Many writers have found themselves in a tough financial situation because they lost an anchor client. It's almost impossible to replace an anchor client overnight. This means it's important to keep an eye on how much of a percentage each client contributes to your overall income.

However, the percentage really depends on your circumstance. My personal rule of thumb is to try to make sure that no single client accounts for more than 20 to 25 percent of my income. I pick this number based on the amount of money I need to make each month. I could get by on 75 percent of my income, if needed. If you must have 90 percent of your income to meet your financial obligations, then you should keep your anchor clients at a lower percentage of your income.

But what should you do if you realize that a client makes up 40 percent of your income or even higher? You aren't just going to drop that client. Or turn down work. You don't want to cause more financial issues trying to prevent something that may or may not happen. Here are three options:

• **Accept the risk and work to mitigate it.** For example, you might build up an emergency fund to make up the difference if you lose the client. I also recommend keeping a close eye out for signs that the company might be making a change or is in financial trouble—your contact leaves, late payments, layoffs, company is bought or an internal reorganization occurs.

• **Decrease the amount of work you take from the company.** The best way to do this is to replace the income with work from another client. You first need to either get a new client or more work from an existing client. Then gradually decrease the amount of work you do with your anchor client. Be sure to give your anchor client notice and be very communicative.

• **Increase your income, which decreases the percentage.** This is my favorite way. For example, if you make $50,000 total and earn $15,000 from one client, then the single client makes up a little more than 30 percent of your income. But if you increase your income so you earn $75,000, then the client drops to only 20 percent of your income. I like this idea because the result is that you have more income and more clients. I will give ideas on how to increase your income in chapter 14.

It's also smart to diversify your client type and industry, in case of economic change. I know several writers who specialized in real estate or construction who lost almost all of their clients during the housing downturn and Great Recession. I try to keep a mix of direct business, agencies and content service companies. And even though my clients are technology based for the most part, I have clients in hospitality and healthcare. This has already proven smart as a lot of my healthcare clients have cut back on content while the industry is in flux.

(!) **Build Your Business:** Look at your list of current anchor clients. Do any of these clients represent a larger portion of your income than you can easily do without or replace? Are you comfortable accepting the risk or do you need to reduce the percentage?

Persistence: Not Giving Up When Most People Would

After I had been freelancing about two years, my phone rang. I almost fell off my chair when I realized that an editor I had been pitching to for the last nine months had CALLED ME out of the blue. I had been successfully publishing in regional parenting magazines around the country, I but heard crickets from our local parenting publication. I did a silent fist pump (or maybe not so silent because I heard her giggle) when she asked me to be a regular contributor.

After I gained my wits, I asked her what about the 31st unsolicited article (yes, I admit I sent that many) made her finally reach out. She laughed and said that she realized I wasn't going away so she'd better at least read an article, then realized the writing was really good. I wrote for her for several years and was able to use many of the stories I wrote for her magazine as clips to help me move to higher-paying markets.

My husband and parents will argue that the quality I am describing is stubbornness, but I prefer persistence. Yes, there is a fine line between persistence and stalking. And yes, it is possible that 31 emails may have crossed the line. But I think the reason it worked instead of turning her off is that each email contained a story idea or a reprint for her publication. I wasn't just bugging her—I was showing her the value I could add.

If I could only give one answer to the question "What is the secret to being a high-income freelancer?" it would be persistence. Freelancing is not easy. You constantly face rejection. You lose clients for reasons that you have no control over. And you always have to be thinking about your next project. I personally think the most successful freelancers have a strong stubborn streak, myself included. You have to want success enough—however you define it—to do what it takes. No one is going to hand it to you. You have to make it happen.

(!) **Build Your Business:** Do you think you are persistent? If not, what would motivate you to be more persistent in building your freelance business? Think about a task for your business that you currently are not being persistent enough in completing. Make a goal and give yourself a small reward when you achieve it. I use taking myself out to lunch—a big treat since I work at home—as a bribe.

Having a Business-Owner Mentality: You Are Not Just a Freelancer

For the first six years that I freelanced, I used to say, "I am a freelance writer," when people asked what I did for a living. But then one day at the beginning of 2015, I changed my answer to, "I own my own freelancing content writing business." I honestly think that those eight words were one of the keys to breaking six figures for the first time in 2015. It wasn't just changing my answer but changing my perception of my career.

Once I began telling people I was a business owner, I started to feel like a business owner. And I started to act like one. Business owners don't try to do everything themselves. They understand what their weaknesses are. So I hired a proofreader. Business owners know that they need to connect with other business owners to stay competitive, so I attended Content Marketing World to meet potential clients. Business owners invest in presenting a professional image so I paid close to $2,000 to redesign my website. And business owners have sales goals, so I set an income goal and actually tracked it.

People who are just casually taking jobs and flying by the seat of their pants aren't typically the writers breaking six figures. It's the ones who do all of the things that I started doing in 2015. But I really think it has to start with a mindset shift that carries through to all of your career decisions.

(!) Build Your Business: Ask yourself if you have the mindset of a freelancer or a business owner. If you answered freelancer, then imagine that a CEO type was put in charge of your freelance career tomorrow. Make a list of things that they would change and do differently. Start small—pick one thing from the list and begin running your business as a business.

(!) Build Your Business: Next time someone asks what you do for a living, answer, "I own my own writing business." Keep saying it until you believe it. Each time you have a decision to make, ask yourself what a business owner would do and then make that choice.

10 Reasons Why You Are Not Meeting Your Income Goals

As part of my quest to understand why a writer earns a high income, I've also paid close attention to the characteristics I see among writers who are struggling to earn a living. Yes, I am positive that there are exceptions, but these are common similarities that I've found—both things that I did during my first six years as a freelancer and habits I've observed in other writers.

If you are still not meeting your income goals, odds are that you are doing one (or more) of the following:

1. You do not constantly market yourself.
It's a familiar story and a trap I've fallen into many times. If you are too busy with work to market yourself, then the project ends and you have no more work.

2. Your marketing is not targeted.
You are not reaching the people who need your specific skills. Or perhaps you're not customizing your approach to the potential client. Maybe you are not presenting yourself in the email in the best way for the client to see how your skills help them. Each outreach needs to be to clients likely to hire you and presented in a way so that they can see exactly why they should hire you.

3. You do not leave your house.
Especially in today's world of emails, tweeting and texting, meeting someone face-to-face cements a relationship. Some of my longest-term clients have been those that I initially met in person.

4. You have a lot of one-off assignments.
The first project with a new client always takes many hours longer than second and third projects with the same client. You have to get used to the client's style, their process and their expectations. This means you make less money on new clients than you do on regular clients.

5. Applying to job ads is your main source of marketing.
If your strategy consists mainly of applying to posted job ads, you're missing a lot of opportunities. When an editor posts a job

ad, they will be inundated with responses—like, hundreds. While I do recommend spending a few minutes each week applying for jobs that you are highly qualified for as part of your overall strategy, it should not be your main source of marketing. You want to be on a potential client's radar before they have a need so that they contact you instead of posting on a job board.

6. You do not follow up with potential clients and past clients.
This is one of the biggest mistakes freelance writers make. The majority of the gigs that I land come on the follow-up. I recently heard of a writer who has been following up with a client for THREE years and was recently offered a huge project. Yes, it can take months or years, but I personally believe that when you don't follow up, you are leaving money on the table.

7. You do not network with other writers.
Other freelance writers are your colleagues, not your competition. Only other freelancers truly understand the ups and downs of this business. Even better, other writers know which editors are looking for work and can often share contacts. Many writers, including myself, regularly refer new clients to other writers.

8. You focus on the per-word rate you earn, rather than what hourly rate you earn through a project fee.
Many writers say that they will only take $1-per-word rates or higher. However, when you compare per-word rates, you are comparing apples to potatoes. It does not account for the amount of work (hours) the project takes.

9. You spend too long working on each project.
The fact is that you only have so many hours to work and if you spend too long on each blog post or article then you will limit the amount of money you can make. I am not talking about turning out crap or cutting corners, but about writing quickly

and turning out good quality work based on the expectations of the client. Even though not every blog post has to be Pulitzer quality, many writers (especially writers who primarily write in top consumer pubs) will spend the same amount of time they spend on high-profile pieces.

10. You do not believe you can make six figures.
If you avoid all of the above mistakes, but don't think in your heart that you can earn a high income, then you most likely will not reach your goal. I firmly believe that this is one of the best and most lucrative times to be a freelance writer. If you think that the work is not out there, then you give yourself permission not to find it instead of being persistent. You have to believe you are good enough and it is possible to earn six figures. And yes, the answer is a wholehearted YES.

① **Build Your Business:** Tell yourself that many other writers are making six figures. There is no reason why you can't be one of these high-earning writers. If you are not meeting your income goals, take some time to think about why.

Breaking Six Figures the First Time

Sometime in late November of 2015, I added up all of my earnings and expected earnings for the year. I knew I was close to six figures, but honestly thought I had fallen short. After earning in the high 50s the previous year, I thought six figures was a pipe dream. But throughout the year, I made a lot of changes to my business and noticed that I was able to land higher-paying clients.

When I realized that I broke six figures, okay, it was only by $300, I did a happy dance in my kitchen while my coworkers (also known as my three dogs—Hank, Katie and Larry) looked at me like I was crazy. I am also very proud of the fact that I made this milestone that year by taking six weeks off work completely and working only about 10 hours a week another four to six weeks while my kids were off school.

My writing buddy Stephanie says that breaking six figures the first time is the hardest because you have to make a lot of changes to your business and develop a certain mentality to get to that level of success. You also have to get rid of habits like settling for low payers and working for clients that don't fit. But she thinks—and I strongly agree with her—that once you break the six-figure mark, it's pretty easy to make $150K or even higher in a year. The painful—and hard part—is getting over $100K the first time.

I spent a lot of time thinking about what I did differently between previous years and 2015. And I've narrowed it down to five things:

1. I had fewer clients.
This may seem counterintuitive since on the surface it is logical to think that you need more clients to make more money. But 2014 was one of my lower years as a freelancer income-wise, and I think it was due to the fact that I had a pile of 14 different 1099 forms from 2014 sitting on my desk in January 2015. When you work on small to medium projects for many different clients, you lose productivity because the first few projects always take longer as you learn the client's expectations, tone and topics. And with fewer clients, you are more likely to develop anchor clients, which as we talked about is key to having more billable hours and a high hourly rate.

2. I developed a high-paying and in-demand niche.
In the first six years as a freelancer I was all over the map—I wrote about parenting, travel, technology, finance, small

business. Pretty much anything that would pay me, I would write about. But in 2015, I developed a niche in data analytics and marketed myself this way through LOIs, LinkedIn and my website. Clients needing this type of expertise began coming to me and I was able to add some big brands to my client list, such as IBM and Hewlett Packard Enterprise. I believe that having these big-name clients in my early days of freelancing helped me land more high-paying clients. Without specializing deeper into the technology niche, I am positive that I would not have broken six figures.

3. I learned to be a better negotiator.
I'm a people pleaser and want everyone to like me. While this trait has been great for developing long-term client relationships, it has also caused me to significantly underprice myself on many occasions. This first step for me was to realize this about myself and be aware that my initial instinct for pricing was most likely too low. I will share more of my tips on negotiating in chapter 14.

4. I only worked with nice people.
I am sensitive (probably one of the most sensitive people you will ever meet) and find it very stressful to work with jerky people. This stress means I get nothing done and am not very nice to be around. The decision to work only with clients that I like was a game changer for me. It made me realize I was in charge and helped me choose projects that were the best fit for me. I explain how to do this in chapter 18.

5. I made time for writing that I enjoy.
For most us being a writer isn't just our job, but also who we are. Writing is our hobby, our stress relief, our therapy and how we give back to the world. But none of these needs are fulfilled when we spend all of our time writing about ROTH IRAs, data analytics or whatever other titillating topics cross your desk. I

began writing personal essays on parenting and remembered how much I loved this type of writing. The pay stunk, but I really think that the fulfillment I got from these stories was a big reason I earned six figures in 2015.

The Numbers Behind a $19K Month

The first time I earned $10,000 in a single month was in the spring of 2016, and I jumped around my kitchen after adding the new numbers. My dogs looked at me like I was crazy. It was a huge milestone for me, and one that I repeated a few times in the fall of 2016.

But when I added up my final tally for February 2017, I was completely silent and shocked. I knew I was having a high-earnings month, but I honestly never expected the number on my FreshBooks accounting system to read $19,550. Yes, that was a single month. And, I even turned down a considerable amount of work.

I think that any writer can achieve this level of financial success if they want to. I'm hoping that by laying out my month in detail you can find something useful to apply to your own business. And that you don't take this as bragging, because it's the furthest thing from the truth. I am sharing these details so that you know it's possible and have a road map of how I did it. It wasn't just one specific tactic or strategy that resulted in my record-breaking month, but rather a lot of things working together. I also want to say that I didn't get to this point overnight or even in a year; this was year nine of my freelancing career.

During February 2017, I worked on 11 different projects with seven different clients, which is slightly higher on both fronts than the average month, but not dramatically. I also worked about 55 hours a week during this month, which included working most weekends because I try to work as little as possible between 2 p.m. and 8 p.m. so I can spend time with my teens. Here is the breakdown of my projects that month:

Project 1: $3,000
Type of Project: Monthly retainer for a four-month annual project (my third year working on it and I landed the gig thanks to my experience working for an accounting firm)
How I Got the Project: The project manager is an ASJA member whom I met through volunteering at a conference.

Project 2: $1,800
Type of Project: Monthly retainer for a healthcare technology project with Agency A
How I Got the Project: I met the owner of the agency at the 2015 ASJA NYC Client Connections event.

Project 3: $2,000
Type of Project: E-book addition to Project 2 (NEW DELIVERABLE FOR EXISTING PROJECT)
How I Got the Project: I suggested an additional deliverable on an existing project.

Project 4: $600
Type of Project: Two blog posts for Agency A and four posts a month going forward (NEW PROJECT)
How I Got the Project: I asked Agency A about additional projects.

Project 5: $2,100
Type of Project: Six blog posts for Agency B at $350 each, which took 3 to 3.5 hours apiece, averaging $100/hour
How I Got the Project: I was on another project for Agency B and asked about additional projects. Once I got on this project, the editor liked my work so much she referred me to another

editor at the very large tech company, which doubled my work from this company.

Project 6: $1500

Type of Project: Ongoing project from Agency B, involving three articles at $500 each, which take about 2.5 hours apiece for an average of $200/hour

How I Got the Project: While working on my original project with Agency B, I heard from another writer about a new project starting with Agency B that was perfect for my experience. I mentioned to my contact at Agency B that I heard about the new project through the freelance grapevine and was interested. They happily added me to the project, which has resulted in $1500 per month since fall.

Project 7: $2,000

Type of Project: Four 700-word articles at $500 each, which took about 4 hours apiece for an average of $125/hour (NEW PROJECT WITH EXISTING CLIENT)

How I Got the Project: Because Agency B knew that I was open to other projects and I had explained my different niches, when a regular writer on a top tech company project left the project, they asked me to take it over.

Project 8: $1,000

Type of Project: Two 700-word articles at $500 each from Agency C, which equates to $150/hour (NEW PROJECT WITH EXISTING CLIENT)

How I Got the Project: Last year an agency I had not worked with before saw my byline from Project 5, which is a high-profile online tech magazine. He approached me for a project and I mentioned my experience writing on several IBM projects and my interest in more work, so he asked me if I wanted to be on a new IBM project. I said yes.

Project 9: $3,000

Type of Project: Whitepaper from content service client in hospitality technology field that took 15 hours and equates to $200/hour (NEW PROJECT)

How I Got the Project: Because my niche of hospitality tech is clearly illustrated on my Contently profile, I was added to a hospitality tech project two weeks before. A last-minute whitepaper revision was offered to the project team and since I had a slow weekend planned, I grabbed it and made some extra cash over the weekend.

Project 10: $1,050

Type of Project: Ongoing agency blogging project. Three 400-word blog posts at $350 each, averaging 1 hour each for $350/hour.

How I Got the Project: I created a portfolio on a content service site and got contacted for this gig about two years later. This is honestly one of my most lucrative projects (rate per hour) and it is one that I could have easily overlooked because the rate seemed low at first glance.

Project 11: $1,500

Type of Project: Specialty publication on a health topic. Two articles, 15 hours at $100/hour.

How I Got the Project: A writer friend passed on this opportunity to me. While not as high paying as some of the others, I really enjoyed this because it was journalistic and about a topic that is personally meaningful.

KEY TAKEAWAYS:
The Secrets behind High-Income Writers

• High-income writers are persistent, have a business-owner mentality and focus on finding (and keeping) anchor clients.

• The way to find anchor clients is to look for clients with long-term needs that are a match for your strengths and personality.

• Try to not let a single client make up a higher percentage of your income than you can either replace quickly or do without for a short term.

• Instead of saying that you are a freelancer writer, reply that you own your own freelance writing business.

Chapter 13

Set Your Rates

A few years ago, I was sitting at a conference talking with a fellow writer who worked for the same online publication as myself. She mentioned to me that she liked the work but didn't like the low pay. I didn't say anything since I thought the pay was fair for the project. Then a few minutes later she mentioned the amount, assuming I was paid the same and I realized that I was making four times the amount as she was for exactly the same type of article.

I didn't know what to do. Should I tell her? Or keep it to myself? Even though I had known the writer all of two hours, I decided to have the tough conversation. She ended up using that information to negotiate a little higher, but because she knew she was being underpaid, she ultimately went to another online publication that ended up being a huge turning point in her career. And the writer turned into my accountability buddy and close friend.

Freelancers Must Talk about Money with Each Other

We've been raised not to talk about money—that it is not polite and that it is a taboo subject. But we are doing a disservice to ourselves, other writers and the freelance writing profession as a whole when we don't talk about money. I used to feel very uncomfortable about sharing financial details with other freelancers but now realize that by talking about money, we help other writers gain the knowledge and the skills they need to support their families through freelancing.

By sharing rate information with each other, we can help each other negotiate higher rates and find out when we are being paid a lower rate than another writer. We give other writers the information that they need to turn down lower-paying assignments, search for the higher-paying gigs and then earn a living wage for their geographic area of the country.

Even more important, when we share our earnings, we help other writers understand what is possible in terms of income potential. By not talking about money, other writers think that low-paying gigs are normal, so they stay there and never move up. Many people, including freelancers, have the starving artist mentality and think that you can only earn a low to average income. But that is not true. I know many six-figure freelancers and a handful who earn over $150K. I never would have known that this level was possible if they hadn't talked about money openly.

Pricing Models: By Word, by Hour or by Project

The first step to negotiating a great rate with a corporate client is to have a solid understanding of the typical pay models and the benefits of each. However, no matter which model your client uses, it is essential for you to accurately estimate how long the piece will take you to complete and calculate how much you are earning per hour to determine if it's actually a good rate.

Pay Per Hour. In this model, you bill the client for a set number of hours at an agreed-upon hourly rate. Many marketing professionals venturing into freelancing seem to prefer this method because it is similar to how agencies often bill clients. While there are some circumstances where this model makes sense, such as a fluid project scope (which means what is required to complete the project keeps changing), I find that this type of pricing makes it harder for freelancers to earn a high income (such as $100 an hour).

The first reason an hourly rate might prevent a freelancer from achieving a high income is that most clients are going to balk at $100 or $150 an hour when it is presented as a straight hourly rate. However, the same client will be fine with an overall project fee that yields $100 an hour (more on that below).

The second reason an hourly rate prevents you from achieving a high income is that you will actually be penalized for becoming more efficient. Let's say you are paid $75 an hour for a weekly article and it typically takes you five hours, which means that you make $375 each week. But after a few months, you become more familiar with the topics, the subject matter experts and the tone, so you now only have to spend four hours on each article, which means that you now make only $300 per week from that client.

A third reason is the administrative work on your part. Tracking hours throughout the day is time-consuming. And many writers, like me, do a lot of writing in their heads while doing other errands or tasks. For the life of me I can't figure out how to bill for that.

I usually explain to clients who want an hourly rate that a project rate makes it easier to budget for their projects. I often add in a line about how I can't figure out how to bill for writing drafts in my head, which usually gets a big laugh.

Pay Per Word. It's pretty straightforward and comfortable for journalists moving into content marketing. If you write 800 words at $1 per word, then you get paid $800. While the gold standard in consumer publications has always been $1 per word, sometimes in content marketing writing, lower-paying per-word rates can actually net you a higher hourly rate, depending on the revision cycle, number of sources, your familiarity with the topics and the amount of research required.

I do not recommend the per-word model because you are not comparing apples to apples. One article might take two hours to research and write whereas a similar article might take ten, depending on what the client needs and expects. When you compare per-word rates in content marketing, you are comparing apples to strawberries. This means you can very easily take a gig that appears to be high paying but takes you a ton of hours. Or on the flip side, you may overlook a gig that appears to be lower paying but takes very little time.

Each of us only has so many hours that we can work. The secret to increasing your income is to increase the amount of money you are earning per billable hour. This is why I recommend ignoring per word and instead focusing on the hourly rate you earn through a project fee.

Pay Per Project. This is the sweet spot. You don't have to track your hours, you can estimate exactly how much you will earn, and you don't have to reveal your actual hourly rate to the client. The best part is that you can increase your income on subsequent projects as you become more efficient. I tell clients that I prefer to price by project because they can more accurately budget for writing projects and I can focus on creating amazing content instead of tracking my hours. When explained this way, most clients will nod their heads and agree.

Continuing the example above, let's say you negotiated a project rate of $500 for the weekly article and the client didn't bat an eye because your $100-an-hour target rate was hidden. A target rate is the amount you want to earn for each hour that you work. This is not the number you tell clients, but a number you need to know for yourself. After all, they don't know how many hours you will spend on the work. When you get the hang of your new gig and it starts taking only four hours, the hourly rate you are earning increases to $125 an hour, which also translates to five free hours a month. You can use these how you wish—take time off, market or do more paying work. But instead of making less money on that particular gig, you essentially make more by increasing your hidden hourly rate.

① **Build Your Business:** Make a list of any current clients that are paying you per word. By using the amount of time that it takes you to complete each project, figure out your hourly rate. If you realize (like I did the first time I did this) that a project you thought was high paying is actually low paying, make a plan to either move to a project fee or drop the client.

Determining How Long a Project Will Take

To evaluate a proposed fee, determine how long the project will take, then divide the number of hours into the proposed fee to see what the hourly rate is. Then compare that to the hourly rate you'd like to earn—your target rate. (More on setting your hourly rate below.)

One of the most important elements of making a good income is being able to accurately determine how long a content marketing deliverable will take you from start to finish. If you consistently underestimate your time, then you will earn a much lower hourly rate. One of the hardest parts of estimating for content marketing writing is that there are many more variables in the process than with writing for traditional publication. Make sure you consider the following eight factors:

1. Are you a fast writer or on the slow side?
Some writers are pretty fast while others are more methodical. From talking with other writers, I have found that one writer may take several hours longer to complete the same project than another writer. Fast writers can take on quantities of lower-paying assignments and still make a good hourly rate, but slower writers need to focus on landing higher-paying assignments. One way to do this is by focusing on higher-paying niches, like technology or finance. It will be harder for a slower writer to earn a good income in niches that are already lower paying, like travel and parenting.

2. What is the length of article?
It's going to take a lot longer to write 1,500 words than 500 words, no matter how you slice it.

3. What is the type of deliverable?
Blogs typically take a lot less time than articles because of the writing style required. Case studies and whitepapers typically take even longer because they must be more polished and formal. Even if the number of sources required are the same, 1,000 words are not created equal across different deliverable types.

4. How many interviews are required? How hard will it be to find quality sources? How long do you think the interviews will last?
A 700-word blog post with only internet research will be much quicker to write than an article where you have to identify, track down and interview two sources. Another factor is how easy or

hard it will be to find a good source on the topic. It is typically much quicker to find an expert on social media than one on ant species native to Brazil. As a general rule, I add an hour to my estimate for each interview required for my content marketing writing projects, but newer freelancers may need more time. Note that I use a transcriptionist so I am not including transcribing time in this estimate.

5. Is the topic one that you are familiar with?
This is another factor that you should weigh heavily into your estimate. It can take me almost twice as long to write an article or blog on a new topic than one that is in my regular niches. If it's a topic that I am familiar with, I know the terminology, I have go-to sources already in my contact list, and I can write the draft a lot quicker.

6. Is the project clearly defined or is the client not totally clear about what they are looking for?
Most editors at traditional publications assign stories all day long and have a good idea of their expectations and scope. But with content marketing writing, you may be working on the very first content marketing project at the company. When a client doesn't really know what they want, the project always takes WAAAAYYYY longer. If I get that feeling up front, I add about 20 percent extra time. Or better yet, don't take the project.

7. How much additional research is required?
Is there documentation you have to read? Do you need to review a number of websites for the article? If you have to read a 30-page study for the report, it is going to take a lot longer than if you only need to read a few paragraphs on a website.

8. How many revision rounds are expected?
Who is involved in the editing process? When you are estimating the project, ask the client about the review process to find out

who will be involved and how many rounds are expected. If it sounds like a lot of people will be involved, I add extra time. If the client mentions that there will be a review by the legal department, then I add even more extra time. Regardless, add additional review time in your estimate to any content marketing projects since the number of review cycles and amount of changes is typically higher in the corporate world than the publishing world.

⊕ **Build Your Business:** Being able to accurately estimate (at least most of the time) how long a project will take is really important. For the next week, estimate how long you think each project you do will take you and then track the actual hours that it takes. Continue this exercise until you are pretty accurate with your estimates.

Setting Your Content Marketing Writing Rates

Here are three steps to determine your project rate for an assignment:

Step 1: Know your target hourly rate.
This is the amount that you aim to earn on all of your writing projects. It's a metric that you need to know for yourself and track. I typically don't tell my clients this rate, but charge project fees instead and aim to earn this amount.

Freelance content marketing writers should try to earn a target rate of at least $100 per hour once you have a year or so of experience under your belt. Journalists and marketing writers should start with at least $100. This is the current going rate for a professional freelancer. If you are earning less than this, then you are underselling yourself.

If you are a relatively new freelance writer and are earning considerably less, then you may want to aim for a lower goal that is more than you are currently bringing in and then move up to $100 incrementally. When I first learned that I should be aiming at $100 per hour, I was earning about $25 per hour. I quickly began looking for projects where I could earn $50 an hour and then moved up to $75 until I finally reached $100.

There are a few exceptions. If you are working on a project requiring specialized knowledge, such as health or technology, then your hourly rate should be higher. If there are very few writers who have the ability to do the project, then my hidden hourly rate is upwards of $300. I regularly earn between $125 and $200 an hour for some of my technology projects that require experience with the technology and the industry.

The trick is that you have to be very conscious of moving up the rate chain and not simply accept the rates that are coming your way. Once I took a proactive approach, I moved from $25 to $100 an hour in about nine months. To move up to a higher rate, you must very consciously look for the higher gigs while getting the clips and experience needed to land those. You are not going to magically move up the pay scale without effort; you must climb up the ladder yourself.

Step 2: Determine how many hours the project will take you. Being able to accurately estimate the time commitment on a project is essential to earning a good hourly rate. By making a habit of estimating each project before you start and then comparing it to how long it actually took you, you will see an improvement in your estimating ability over time. See chapter 13 for how to figure out how long a project will take.

Step 3: Do the math.
Multiply your desired hourly rate by the estimated time that it will take you in order to determine how much you should earn

on the piece to meet your business goals. Then do more math (I know, I hate math as well) to compare the pricing that the client is giving you on the project.

(!) **Build Your Business:** Set your target hourly rate. If you are not yet earning at least $100, then pick a rate higher than you are currently earning. For example, if you are currently earning $25 an hour, begin pricing your projects to earn $50 an hour, then $75 and then $100.

(!) **Build Your Business:** Next time you are asked your rates, use this method to provide a quote to a potential client. If the number seems high, take a breath. You are worth being paid competitive rates.

Should You Ever Take an Unpaid Writing Test?

In the past few months, I have been asked several times to write a test article for free when applying for a freelance job. While I don't have a problem with writing/editing tests for full-time employees since the company is making a long-term and expensive commitment, I don't think that companies should ask freelancers to take unpaid writing tests. Interestingly enough, editors for consumer publications never ask this of writers, so it is a relatively new dilemma for many content marketing writers. I believe that this unfortunate trend is due to many companies translating their staff hiring process to the freelance world where it doesn't fit.

While I am fundamentally opposed to companies asking writers to do a writing test and wish that all writers could turn down the "opportunity," I realize that we don't live in a perfect world and writers need to feed their families. There are a few cases where it can be the right decision to do it. Most of the time writers should turn it down and run for the hills. I will admit that in a very few cases, I have done the writing test after careful thought to my business goals and current workload as well as the potential income of the opportunities.

Before you get to the point of deciding about that unpaid test work, here are five strategies to try to get the client to change their mind. If these don't work, then you will have a decision to make.

- **Tell the client that you don't typically do unpaid writing tests for freelance gigs.**
Ask what they are trying to learn through the test. Explain that if they called a plumber that they wouldn't ask them to fix their toilet for free to see if they could do a good job.

- **Offer the client writing samples in the form of your previously published articles and deliverables.**
Ask your client if they would like you to send additional samples, especially for work that closely resembles the tone, content and deliverable of their project.

- **Point your clients to recommendations from your past clients.**
If you have recommendations on your LinkedIn profile or a testimonial page on your website, make sure that your prospective client has seen your endorsements.

- **Show an unedited draft.**
Clients sometimes want to see a writer's work before it has been edited. This is a common reason that clients ask for the writing tests. Point them to your own blog or an unedited draft of a published piece. Make sure that it is not a piece that is awaiting publication, because you might be violating your contract with that client by sharing work that hasn't been made public.

- **Suggest starting with a small paid project, such as a blog post.**

Explain that this gives the client the chance to evaluate your work on a trial basis without a long-term commitment on their part while you are still compensated for your valuable time. I have had pretty good success with this strategy.

If you're a new freelancer without clips to show, then you may need to take the writing test. It is very hard to get gigs without clips. Sometimes even with loads of clips, experienced writers find clients that won't budge on the writing test. You have to then make the decision to either do it or walk away. Think about what else you would be spending the time doing, how badly you need the work and the odds of you landing the gig. If you are just starting out, have zero paying work at the time, and are very confident that you are a perfect match for the client, then it may be a good calculated risk.

KEY TAKEAWAYS:
Set Your Rates

- With project pricing, you have the ability to earn a higher income as you become more efficient with a project or client.

- With per-hour pricing, you learn less money as you get more efficient with the project, which makes no sense to me.

- Always know the hourly rate you are likely to earn on a project.

- Aim to earn at least $100 per hour—or higher for technical projects.

• Be wary of comparing projects based on per-word rates because the time required to complete the project may vary wildly.

• Interviews can significantly decrease your hourly rate. Clarify the number of interviews before negotiating.

Chapter 14

Negotiating with Clients

I was on the phone with a potential client and was negotiating a new project. I originally quoted $400 for a blog post. But within 12 seconds had been talked down to $200 for the post. When I hung up the phone my son (who was seven at the time) asked me why I was worth $200 less at the end of the call than the beginning. Ouch. That was a turning point for me and I vowed to become a better negotiator.

I wish I could say that I've turned into a fantastic negotiator, but that would be a lie. I have become a better negotiator, though. It will never be my biggest strength. But at least it's been a while since I've told a client that I want to do the project so badly that I will take whatever rate they pay. Or got in an argument with a client that they were paying me too much. Yes, as much as I wish I could say these were fictional examples, they are totally true. I am really that terrible of a negotiator.

Negotiating a good rate is more challenging with content marketing writing than other types of freelance writing. I think it's because there are so many variables between projects and client expectations. It can be difficult to immediately tell the difference between a high-paying job and a low-paying job due to all the variables.

For example, a $350 blog post can be a great rate if the assignment is for 400 words, requires no interviews and summarizes a recent industry study. That same rate can be a very low rate if the deliverable is 1,000 words, requires two interviews and the revision process requires several rounds of approval. In the same way, a 3,000-word whitepaper that pays $1 per word (a potentially attractive rate) but takes you 50 hours because of multiple interviews, heavy revision requests and hours of research ends up not being as lucrative as it looks at first.

After spending the past few years writing mainly content marketing deliverables and talking about the topic of rates with hundreds of writers, I can attest that there are definitely content marketing gigs out there that will earn you at least $100 an hour. So next time you are tempted to take a lower-paying content marketing gig, keep looking. Just like with consumer and trade publications, it takes persistence, marketing and time to land the higher-paying clients.

When an editor for a trade or consumer pub hires you, they typically tell you how much they will pay per word most of the time and there is little negotiating since the publication works with freelancers all day long. However, when working with corporate clients, the pay model is not nearly as cut-and-dried so typically there is more room for negotiation.

Evaluating a Rate

Often, a client will offer you a project and specify the rate they want to pay. It's easy to think that a project is too low paying when in fact you can earn a great hourly rate or—the flip side— thinking that because a client quotes a high number that it is indeed a high-paying project on a per-hour basis.

I recently worked on a project where I was paid $300 apiece for 500-word blog posts. On the surface, this seems to be low paying. But I asked the client what was involved and found out that the client provided the story ideas, the stories required no interviews and the topics were a subject I was very familiar with. I took four of the stories and found that I could complete all four in about 2.5 hours because they were very quick to write. The client pretty much accepted the stories as-is, and I had very few revisions. My paycheck was $1200 for these four stories, which ended up being $480 an hour.

On the other hand, I did a content project a few years ago that paid $1.75 per word, netting me $1700 for a 1,000-word story, which at first glance seemed like a high-paying project. But the story ended up requiring 10 interviews, a rigorous fact-check process and several revisions. I spent about 35 hours on the project, which worked out to an hourly rate of $48.57.

If you take only one thing away from this book, remember that when a client offers you a project, it's essential to ask questions and do the math to figure out if the rate is high or low. First impressions are often deceptive.

Answering the "What Are Your Rates?" Question

The other way that a negotiation starts is with a client asking you what your rates are. For me, "What are your rates?" is an impossible question to answer because my rates depend on so many factors. I can't say what I charge for a blog post, because my rates for a 400-word blog post with no interviews on a non-technical subject are typically around $300 to $350. However, I charge $500 to $700 for an 800-word blog post on a technical subject that requires an interview.

I respond back and ask them to describe a typical project (type of deliverable, length, number of sources) and let them know I am happy to give a ballpark estimate based on those specifications. If the client responds that they haven't used freelancers before and don't really know what they need, then I will request a phone call to talk through their needs in more detail.

Three Ways I Negotiate

As I've said, I don't love negotiating. I worry that the client won't like me and that they'll take their project and go home. But over the years, I've learned that my fear of a great client walking away was unfounded. If someone couldn't meet my rate requirements, then we weren't a match anyway. Working for them would have cost me money because it would have meant that I was missing out on higher-paying work or looking for a new client that would pay my rates. When negotiating, I now do these three things:

1. If a client names a price first, I always counter with a slightly higher price. I usually go about 10 to 20 percent higher for my counter offer, depending on the rate. For example, if a client offers $300 for a 500-word blog post with no interviews and no ideation (they come up with story ideas), then I will counter at $350. If someone offers me $1,500 for a case study, I might counter at $1,750 or $2,000.

2. If a client asks me to name my price, then I come up with my estimate and then force myself to add 10 to 20 percent to the rate. This compensates for my tendency to underbid and gives me padding for negotiation.

3. If I start a project and it ends up being more work than I estimated when I negotiated the rate, I go back to the client and ask for a higher rate. Each time I have done this, I am very specific about the tasks that are taking longer and why this justifies a higher rate. Sometimes they say no. But often they say yes. And even if they say no, I have lost absolutely nothing. And the additional money I have earned for the same amount of work over the past two years has made it worth a few moments feeling uncomfortable.

Tips for Negotiating with Clients

If you struggle with negotiating for rates, you are not alone. Many writers are uncomfortable with negotiating. Here are a few tips that have worked for me:

• **Try to get the client to name a price first.** This is the best way to make sure that you are not underpricing yourself.

• **Quote a slightly higher price than what feels comfortable.** You can always reduce your rates, but you can't increase them. One of the worst feelings is when a client accepts your rates immediately and you know you undersold yourself.

• **Ask another writer for their opinion before quoting the client.** Getting another writer's input often gives me the confidence to increase my rate. I recently ran a quote by another writer and she told me I that I should be charging double what I was proposing. And she was right—the client responded back with "Works great for us" within seven minutes, which means I should have quoted even higher.

• **Do not quote a price on the phone.** I am a terrible negotiator over the phone. But I am much bolder if I get off the phone, think about it and then email the client. I almost always undercut my rates on the phone, and I feel more confident asking for higher rates via email.

• **Reduce the scope for clients with fixed budgets.** If a client has a fixed budget that is below your rates, but you want to work with them, consider using the scope as a means to negotiate. Scope refers to what the client requires, such as word count, number of interviews, amount of research. When you lower the amount of work that is required for you, then it increases your hourly rate. For example, a potential client wanted me to write an 800-word article on a technical subject with three interviews for $600. I estimated the project would take me five hours, which was an hourly rate lower than my target rate of $150 for technical topics. The client was unable to raise the rate to $800 so I asked if we could change the scope to one interview and web research, which I estimated would take me three-and-a-half hours and result in a $171-per-hour rate.

• **Don't worry about losing a potential client by quoting too high.** I hear this concern all the time. Honestly, if your quote is slightly higher than what a client expects or can afford, they will negotiate with you. If your rate is much higher than their budget, then they were not a good fit for you because you were too far apart. Every time I've taken a low-paying client, it hasn't been a great experience because I have a feeling of resentment from the start. Quote what you are worth. The clients who need your specialized skills and experience will be willing to pay.

When you are just starting out and don't yet have deep expertise, you may have to take a few lower-paying gigs. But just be sure not to stay there thinking that you need three years writing on projects making $25 an hour to become an expert. You need to quickly transition out of the poverty mindset and begin pursuing better-paying gigs. You may not land the big names right out of the gate. But you can quickly move into medium-sized brands and start heading up the ladder. Keep the confidence that you are worth more than the lower-paying and put in the time to find the better-paying projects.

⊙ **Build Your Business:** Think about how you are currently negotiating with clients. Do you think that you are doing a good job? How could you improve negotiation in the future? Make a list of three things you are going to do differently next time you are trying to land a new gig.

⊙ **Build Your Business:** Ask a freelance writer friend if they would be willing to be a sounding board next time you are trying to estimate a project. This way you know exactly who to call (or email) next time you are doing an estimate.

When to Take a Slightly Low-Paying Gig

You will hear some freelancers say that experienced writers should never take work that's less than $1 per word or $100 an hour. However, the world is not black and white. And there are times when you may find yourself considering taking a lower-paying project. And sometimes that really is the right business decision. I do think that it should be a very conscious decision made with a business-owner mindset, not just saying yes because someone is offering you work.

I am not talking about taking a project earning $100 for 1000 words with three interviews. But a well-known brand with an ongoing need for content that is offering $200 for 600 to 700 words or $500 for 1000 words with a couple of interviews might be worth considering. Here are three situations where taking a low payer may be the right choice:

1. You are in danger of not paying your bills or being able to feed your family. You have to do what you have to do and no one should judge you for whatever projects you have to take to get by. However, it's easy to fall into the trap of low-paying projects and constantly working. If you take low-paying projects because of a financial emergency, come up with a plan to get back on track where you can spend the time to market for higher-paying clients.

2. The project feeds your soul. Two years ago, I wrote several essays around 1000 words for 100 bucks, which is really low. But I loved writing the essays and it made me happy. I like to say that some projects pay your mortgage while others feed your soul. And it's important to have a balance of both. Ideally, your passion projects should also be competitively paying. However, sometimes they aren't. And as long as it's a conscious decision and you know why you are taking the gig, then it's totally fine.

3. You can use the clips or brand names to get more clients in the future. When I look back on the last six years of freelancing, I can point to working for American Express OPEN Forum and Entrepreneur.com as turning points in my career because having these clips helped me land other clients. However, I stayed in the OPEN Forum gig for over two years and likely missed out on other higher-paying gigs. I should have written for the website for three to four months, gotten some great clips and then moved on.

ⓘ Build Your Business: Think about a time in the past where you have taken a lower-paying gig. Do you think that it was the right move? What should you have done differently?

Why I Don't Let Low Rates Upset Me

I have read many posts and heard many conversations about writers frustrated with clients offering low rates. While I understand that it can feel discouraging, I have seen too many writers stop looking for content gigs because they think they are all low paying. Other writers get discouraged and insulted when they run across the bottom feeders.

While this isn't a new problem—many regional and national journalistic publications are low payers—I do think that there are more low-paying clients in content. I think the reason is that it's easy to find low-paying content gigs—just cruise Craigslist or head over to Upwork. It doesn't take much effort, targeting or searching. This makes it easy to think that high-paying gigs are few and far between.

I personally don't think that is the case at all. If anyone can write about the topic and anyone can find the gig, then the client doesn't have to pay much. But when you specialize in areas requiring expertise and reach out directly to the clients and agencies, then the rates are in a totally different ballpark.

So next time you run across a low-paying gig, take a breath and move on. I promise you can do this and there are higher-paying gigs are out there. It's just up to you to find the clients.

Negotiating Legal Documents with Clients

It's easy to think just about money when you think about negotiating, but you can also negotiate legal terms. When you and a client agree to work together, the next step is often signing legal documents, including a contract and possibly a non-disclosure agreement.

Contracts and Indemnification Clauses

I tend to be overly trusting, but I have learned through other writers the importance of both always having a contract and making sure that the contract does not set you up for a potential costly lawsuit in the future. When I first started freelancing, I would take work without a contract, which leaves you open to the client deciding not to pay you or changing the requirements for payment. But with a contract you have a legally binding document. Now I never work without a contract.

Some clients send me a contract for each piece that I do while others have a general contract that is in effect for all of the work that we do together. I personally prefer a general contract and then agree to rates through email for additional projects, but that is partly because I am terrible about forgetting to send back signed documents. Other writers I know prefer a separate contract for each piece.

Most content marketing gigs are work-for-hire. This means that everything you write belongs to the company and you are selling all rights to the article. You can't sell it as a reprint later. This is one of the reasons that many content gigs pay higher than journalism because you cannot earn additional income on the article after it is published.

The first time I was handed a contract full of legal language, I assumed that I had two choices, either sign it or not work with the client. But through ASJA and Freelance Success, yes that's another plug for both, I have learned that it is possible to negotiate contract terms with clients. Of course, some will say no, but many writers have shared that they have successfully gotten contracts changed to more freelance-friendly terms.

The biggest thing to watch out for is an indemnification clause, which specifies who has to pay losses, damages, settlement fees and attorney fees if someone sues the company based on something that you wrote. The severity of the indemnification clause can vary, with the worst ones for freelancers saying that you are liable even if the claim is proven to be unfounded. Some indemnification clauses are written so that you are responsible even if someone threatens to sue. This means you could have to pay even if it is proven in court that what you wrote was accurate.

If you are faced with a contract containing an indemnification clause, ask to have it changed so that the clause is only in effect after legal harm has been proven in a court of law, by judgment sustained, after all appeals have been exhausted. You should also ask to have the phrase "to the best of the writer's knowledge" added to the clause whenever possible. This way you are only responsible if you have knowingly done something wrong.

Contracts are hard and confusing. One of the benefits of belonging to the American Society of Journalists & Authors (ASJA) is that members can ask the Contracts & Conflicts committee for help with contracts. This committee is very knowledgeable and helpful. Yes, this is a shameless plug.

(!) **Build Your Business:** Look at a contract that you have recently signed. Did you unknowingly sign an indemnification clause? If this is a client that issues contracts for each project, ask the client to make changes for the next contract to make it more freelance friendly.

Non-Compete Clauses
A non-compete can be a separate document or a clause within the contract. It basically specifies that, for a certain period of time, you cannot write on the topic or work with competitors. Think very carefully before signing a non-compete clause since you are very likely limiting your future earnings. As freelancers,

our business depends on our ability to get clients in the future and a document limiting that ability can lower our future income.

If the client insists on a non-compete and you decide that the limitations are worth the benefit, then you should negotiate as much as possible. Try to get as short of a time as you can—a non-compete for three months is not going to cause as many headaches as one that follows you around for three years.

If the non-compete states that you cannot write on the same topic for the specified time, get the terms as specific as possible. Let's say that you wrote an article for a client about a new treatment for diabetes and signed this type of non-compete. Does this mean that you cannot write about this specific treatment or is the clause referring to diabetes? Even worse, could the client come back and say that it referred to any health topic? By having the specific limitations spelled out as much as possible, you are clear on what you are agreeing to so you can make an informed decision.

Some non-competes also state that you cannot work with competing companies during the time period noted. Every time I have been asked to sign this type of document, I request that the client specify exactly which clients they consider competitors. This makes it easier for me to really assess the odds of me wanting to work with those specific companies and make an informed decision.

(!) **Build Your Business:** Look at your contracts with all current clients and look specifically for any non-compete clauses that you have already signed. If you are unsure of any restrictions, check with your client to make sure you don't accidentally break the clause. And if you realize that a contract is too restrictive or not clear, ask the client if they would issue a new and revised contract.

Non-Disclosure Agreements (NDA)

These are very common in content marketing and I've been asked to sign many. Some potential clients require that I sign an NDA before they will even talk with me about the possibility of working together. NDAs can vary widely from stipulations that say you cannot share company secrets, to others that insist you not even tell anyone that you worked for the client.

Read the clauses carefully to make sure that you are okay following the terms. One contract I had required that my computer be password protected on a secure wireless network with the latest version of an anti-virus software when working on their projects. Another specified that any printed documents related to company projects had to be stored in a locked drawer or file cabinet.

Another thing to look for is brands that specify that you are not allowed to use their name or clips for marketing purposes. This means your only value from the project will be actual money that you earn, so make sure the rates are worth the effort. When I was trying to move up to bigger clients, I was considering taking a lower-paying gig with a well-known company. After reading the NDA, I realized that I could not put the clips on my website or even tell future clients that I had written for the brand. Because this was my main reason for settling for a lower rate, I ended up turning down the gig.

(!) **Build Your Business:** Look at any NDAs that you have with any current clients. Make sure that you are following everything that is outlined in the agreement. Check with the client if you have any questions.

202 · THE FREELANCE CONTENT MARKETING WRITER

When Negotiations Fail

My personal experience is that when I have to spend a lot of time negotiating with a client, they usually tend to wind up being one of my least favorite clients. The reason is that if they feel they are paying a really high rate, then they want something that is the most amazing piece of content in the universe. While I know that you are great, no one can be perfect. When a client feels like they are overpaying in their mind, they tend to be super picky. I have found it is a much better use of my time to look for clients that have no issues paying my rate instead of try to convince someone to pay me a higher rate.

How to Walk Away

Even after all of these years of freelancing, I almost always manage to convince myself (usually at 3 a.m., which is a terrible time to make business decisions) that if I turn down the gig, then I will never ever get work again. This of course is totally false, but it's easy to feel like you are making a mistake. This is why I think it's so important to have a target hourly rate and determine the estimated hourly rate you will earn on a project. When you have a number to compare, then it makes it an easier decision. Note I said easier—an accountant might think it's easy, but us writers see all the shades of gray in everything.

I also recommend walking away if you cannot get the client to modify unfriendly non-compete clauses and contracts. Sometimes clients will not change their contracts, but it is definitely worth trying because I have heard many stories of writers successfully getting contracts modified.

So you have now decided that you need to turn down the client. How do you do it? I personally prefer saying no over email because, on the phone, I have more than once been convinced by a client to take a lower-paying job when I had started the conversation with the intent of saying no.

Here is a sample email that I send:

Hi (client you're turning down),

I enjoyed talking with you last week about your project and learning about your needs. After thinking about the project and the rate, I have decided that the proposed rate does not meet my business goals. If you have any projects in the future that have a higher rate, let me know. I would love to work together in the future on another project.

Jennifer

I have found that the phrase "does not meet my business goals" feels comfortable to me, sounds professional and is something that a client can understand. It also doesn't put the client on the defensive by telling them that the rate is too low per se. Interestingly enough, I have had many clients respond to me after I sent this email that they will keep me in mind for higher-paying projects. And guess what, FOUR times it has worked out. An agency got a higher-paying client or the editor moved to another company that paid higher rates. I personally feel good about ending it this way and leaving the door open for the future.

However, you should come up with the phrasing that feels most comfortable to you and is authentic to your personality and how you run your business.

It takes courage. It takes gumption. But turning down low-paying clients is the only way to make room in your schedule to find and work with the great-paying clients. And once you hit the send button, I promise you are not doomed. You will find another higher-paying client. And usually it happens much sooner than you think.

(!) **Build Your Business:** Think about your current clients and ask if you should have walked away from any of these clients. Note the warning signs that you saw during the negotiation process so you can spot issues next time.

KEY TAKEAWAYS:
Negotiating with Clients

• Before accepting a gig, know the hourly rate you are likely to earn.

• If you are a timid negotiator, send your estimates over email instead of negotiating over the telephone.

• Ask another writer for their thoughts when quoting and negotiating with a client.

• Be willing to walk away from low-paying clients.

• Taking a low-paying client can cost you money because you will not be available (or looking) for higher-paying work.

Chapter 15

Increasing Your Income

It took me several years to realize that, unlike when I worked at a company, my boss wasn't going to just give me a raise. I kept thinking that high-income projects just fell into other writers' laps because they had something that I didn't have. Maybe they were a better writer, or perhaps they were in a better niche. I thought it was easy for everyone but me, since most people only share their highlight reel and not the dark moments.

Then one day I realized that I was the boss. And that I had the power to give myself a raise. As soon as I realized that I was in charge of my own income and began strategically working to make more money, things changed. My yearly earnings increased from $30K to $50K to over six figures within just a few years. It wasn't luck. It wasn't that I had suddenly become a better writer. The reason my earnings doubled was that I made the conscious decision to actively increase my income and then did the work to make it happen.

The first thing I did was look at what the high-income writers were doing that I wasn't doing. As I talked about in chapter 12, I began focusing on anchor clients and developing a business mindset. I was born stubborn—or persistent—so I didn't need any work in that area. Before you begin following the steps below to actively increase your income, I recommend reviewing the three characteristics in chapter 12. Without being persistent, having a business mindset and focusing on anchor clients, it will be challenging (but not impossible) to increase your income. Here are the seven steps that I used to increase my income:

Step 1: Know Where You Are

You can't increase your income unless you know exactly where you are right now and why you are earning this amount. Set some time aside and gather the following information:

- How much you earned last year
- How much you have currently earned this year
- Your average hourly rate
- How many hours you work on average each week
- The average hourly rate you earn from each client
- The percentage of your income each client represents

Don't analyze this information now or let yourself get discouraged. Simply put on your researcher hat and gather the data.

Step 2: Set Your Income Goal

I've seen a number of discussions on writer forums and Facebook groups where writers share that they do not have an income goal. The typical reason given is that it's hard to set a goal because they don't know how much work they are going to land in a year. I think that this sets you up to earn less money than you are otherwise could. The same could be said of any business, but you don't see businesses taking the "whatever comes my way" approach. Without actively tracking your income against a target, you don't know if you need to make changes to your strategy or approach.

Decide how much money you want to make this year.
You probably already know the number. Keep your previous earnings in mind as well as how many hours you want to work. Yes, you want to increase your income, but you also have to make realistic leaps. For example, if you earned $30,000 last year and only want to work 25 hours a week then you should probably aim for $60,000 this year instead of $100,000.

I usually pick a minimum goal and a stretch goal. For example, your minimum goal might be $80,000, but your stretch goal is $100,000. Keep in mind that you can (and should) reevaluate and change your goal throughout the year.

Step 3: Figure out how much money you need to earn on a weekly and monthly basis.
I'm not an analytical person. But I found knowing how much I needed to make each week and month to be the turning point in being able to take control of my income. There are five steps to setting this goal and using it to make more money:

• **Decide how many weeks you want to take off for vacation.** Zero is not an acceptable answer. I'll give you plenty of tips in chapter 19 on how to take vacations as a freelancer, so for right now just give a realistic number.

• **Determine your monthly income target.** Divide your income goal by 12 to determine the amount you need to earn each month. If your vacation will be spread through the year, then this gives you a rough amount. For example, if you want to earn $100,000, then you will need to earn $8,333 each month. However, I pretty much take the entire month of December off, so I divide my goal by 11. This means that if I want to make $100,000 then I must earn $9,090 each month.

• **Determine your weekly income.** Divide your income goal by the number of weeks you want to work. For example, if you want to make $100,000 and take four weeks off either as sick time or vacation time then you need to earn $2,083 each week.

• **Track your income goal.** I used to keep track of this in my head. But last year I started using FreshBooks and it was so much easier. I know other writers that use a Google sheet or Excel spreadsheet. I count the work that I finish in the week that I file it, which may or may not be the same as I invoice. Other people count it when they invoice. It really doesn't matter as long as you are consistent.

• **Make changes to your marketing as needed.** If I see that I'm off my monthly goal or haven't made my weekly goal in a few weeks, then I know that I need to make a change. My first line of defense is contacting current and recent clients to see if they have any work. If that doesn't drum up the business that I needed, then I start marketing to businesses and agencies.

Step 4: Drop Your Lowest-Paying (or Biggest PITA) Client
This is difficult to do, but if you keep low-paying clients, then you will never earn your income potential. Many writers try to find a higher-paying gig to replace a lower-paying client without cutting that client loose first. This often does not work because you do not have the time to do the marketing needed while you're still working at the lower rate. You also don't feel as much pressure to find a new client so you often hang on much longer than you should. Here are three steps to dropping your lowest-paying client:

• Look at the list of hourly rates that you wrote down for each client and circle your three lowest-paying clients based on an hourly rate.

• Look at each one and think about their PITA factor as well as the percentage of your overall income that they represent. You do not want to drop a client that is more than 20 percent of your income without careful planning. After thinking about all the factors, decide which client to drop. If you have several low-paying clients that represent just a small portion of your income, consider dropping all of them because each client takes project management time that you can use to look for other work.

• Contact the client and let them know that you will no longer be available or will have reduced availability. I usually tell the client that I recently got a big project and am not going to have the availability to work on their projects after X day. If you would be willing to keep the client if they raised your rates, then tell them that their rates no longer meet your business goals. Keep the email short, sweet and professional.

Step 5: Raise Your Rates with Existing Clients
If you have ongoing work with clients you have had for a while and the rates are typically lower than you are earning for other clients, another strategy is to notify the client that you are increasing their rates after a certain date. Many writers use the beginning of the year as a starting point for new rates since this is a model that businesses are used to seeing.

The first time I did this, I stressed myself out majorly and decided if I did it that all my clients would fire me and I would never work again. But of course, that didn't happen. And several times, my client actually responded that they had been meaning to give me a raise themselves.

The way you raise your rates depends on the payment method you are using with the client. If you are charging the client for regular work on a project basis, such as a set of blog posts, you should let the client know the new rate. Here's a sample email to raise your rates.

Hi Steve,

I hope you had a nice time on vacation last week—I'm jealous. I have really enjoyed working with your agency over the past three years and hope to continue for a long time to come.

I wanted to let you know that I am raising my rates starting January 1, 2019. I will be charging $50 more per blog post, so your monthly fee for the four posts will be $1600. Let me know if you have any questions or want to chat on the phone.

Jennifer

Step 6: Charge New Clients Your New Targeted Hourly Rate
For me the easiest way to increase my income is to simply quote higher prices when I get new clients. I also began targeting medium and national brands instead of small businesses and local brands since they would be more likely to pay higher rates. Then when you set your rates, as described in chapter 13, use the new higher-target hourly rate that you came up with in step 2. And then have the belief in yourself that you deserve competitive rates and to walk away from lower payers.

Step 7: Add In-Demand Niches That Require Specialized Knowledge
Yes, I know that I have already talked a bunch about niches. But it bears mentioning again in this chapter because certain niches pay higher rates and it is a very smart strategy to add high-paying niches. It's an easy way to increase your income. Reread chapter 3 to help find higher-paying niches, especially the sections about adding both B2B and technology angles to your current niche to increase your income.

My general rule of thumb is that niches that have a lower number of writers available are going to pay higher. And typically, the reason there are fewer writers in this space is because it requires specialized knowledge gained through years of experience.

I recently ran a proposed quote by a fellow writer for a white-paper on virtualized networks in the healthcare industry and she told me to double my price. I told her I was worried that they would go hire someone else. She responded, "There are only a handful of writers that specialize in this topic with the national brand experience that they want. And two of them are on this phone call. Who else are they going to call? They will pay it." And she was right. In fact, when the client emailed me three minutes after I sent my quote with "Sounds great. Let's get started," I realized I could have gone even higher.

How to Increase Your Income By $15,000 (or More) This Year without Working One Hour More

I've given you the overall roadmap for increasing your income. But none of these are quick fixes or overnight answers. Instead, I gave you the long-term strategy to earn more money and keep earning more money. So now I want to talk about three relatively easy things that you can start doing right away that can make a big difference in your pay.

Always Ask for More Money
I wish I knew who gave me the advice so I could give credit. But many years ago, a writer shared with me that no matter what rate the client offered, she always countered with a slightly higher rate, even if the gig was already high paying. She told me that many clients build some leeway into the rate they offered so that

they can negotiate. And that by not negotiating, I was leaving money on the table that the client was planning to pay me.

So I tried it. And it worked, really well. Most of the time, the answer was yes. And the few times it was no, they still hired me. The worst that happened was the client said no. But I realized quickly that this one move had a dramatic and compounding effect for long-term clients. A new client offered me $350 for a 700-word blog post and I countered that I usually earned $500 for the same amount of work. The answer was a yes. The client turned out to be an anchor client that was worth over $30,000 to me in 2017. I calculated that I increased my income by $9,000 simply by sending a single email.

A good rule of thumb is asking for 20 percent more than offered, then negotiating down if necessary. So if a client offers you $250 for a 300- to 400-word blog post, counter with $300, which is 25 percent more. And if the project is a whitepaper and the client throws about $3000 for the fee, then counter with $3600.

Payoff: If you get $50 more on four posts/articles a week, that adds up to $10,400 over a year. If you negotiate like this on every assignment, the payoff is likely to be much higher.

(!) **Build Your Business:** Next time you land a new client or an existing client offers you a new project, ask for more money. Make it an automatic part of your process and do it every single time.

Increase Your Writing Speed

Most writers who earn a good income, especially content marketing writers, are fast writers. Writers who tell me that they are struggling to reach their income goals confess to being on the slow side.

You only have so many hours to work and you can only charge your clients so much. So there is a limit to how much you can control those two variables. But you do have control over how long each article takes you. Writing faster improves your hourly rate (assuming you bill per project as I recommend). The good news is that you can learn to write articles faster, which increases the number of articles you can write, and in turn increases your income potential.

I am in no way talking about turning in crap or low-quality writing. Instead I am talking about using your time productively as well as making strategic business decisions. Improving writing speed is one of the most important (and easiest) things writers can do to increase their income. All of the other ways to increase your income—finding new clients and earning higher rates—are harder to control. But how long something takes you to write is totally within your control.

Here are 10 ways to write faster:

• **Write a bad first draft.** Next time you sit down to write an article, don't think about making it good, don't think about getting everything perfect. Just get the words out as quickly as possible. Then, go back into the draft (preferably the next day, but a few hours of distance will do in a pinch) and edit, rework and polish it. For me, this saves hours. The quality is better because I simply write the first draft without overthinking it.

• **Walk away.** If I am struggling with a piece, then I stop working on it. Nothing wastes more time than staring at a screen. Instead, I will work on another project. Or I will go play on social media or take a walk for a few minutes to clear my head. Often, I find that relaxing and taking a break will help me write faster after I come back.

• **Write in your head.** I often write entire articles in my head while driving or running or waiting in the carpool line. I can really increase my hourly rate when I do this, because when I come back to my computer, all I basically have to do is transcribe what is in my head. Of course, I go back and edit it heavily. The trick is that I have to get to my computer quickly after I write it in my head to "get it out," and I can't work on anything else until I get this particular article out of my head. But as I have gotten older, I have learned to succumb to the oddities of my brain instead of fighting them, which has been a huge key in writing faster.

• **Find your best time of the day to write first drafts.** I am a morning person, so that is the time where I do the work that I need to think about: editing, research, etc. But oddly enough, sometimes my best first drafts come in the evening when I am tired. I will just write quickly and most productively because I am "looser." Yes, and this may sound odd, I have also found that a glass of red wine can sometimes help my productivity—assuming I have time to edit before sending it the editor. Figure out when your body rhythm is best for writing and go with it, no matter how odd it seems.

• **Write to the quality the project and client needs.** There is a big space between writing a crappy article and writing something that is Pulitzer worthy. I never turn in something that I am not proud of. But if you are writing a $300 blog post on using social media, then every word does not need to be a masterpiece. The readers don't need this level of writing and your client doesn't expect it. Tailor your results to the level of quality that is needed for each project and then give your client a little more than they expect.

• **Outsource.** Think about what tasks you do that you could pay someone less than you make per hour to handle. I am a terrible proofreader. It takes me forever to proof my own work, and even then, I miss stupid typos, so I outsource proofreading to a virtual assistant. I do the same with my initial research; my VA will find me a list of articles, surveys and sources based on the topic for me to use as a starting point. This saves me hours. And since I pay my VA less than the $100 to $150 I aim to make per hour, the math works out in favor of outsourcing whenever possible.

• **Write about familiar topics.** I can whip out an article on almost any data analytics topic in no time. But if you ask me to write about lifestyle topics, it will take me hours and hours. I am not as knowledgeable in this area so I spend more time researching, and I am simply not as comfortable writing on home and garden type stuff. With tech, I know where to look online for good information, I have some go-to sources, I know the knowledge level of my audience and I know the terminology. So while this is the opposite for most people, I can write about tech stuff faster than I can lifestyle. The point is that when you write in an industry and on topics that you are an expert in, it takes you less time to complete the project.

• **Write groups of blog posts in batches.** Each time you switch projects, it takes time. You have to shift gears, shift audiences and shift tone. If you have a client that you do a number of short pieces for on a regular basis, try to write these pieces all at once. So if you do weekly blog posts for a client, once a quarter spend two days knocking out all 12 of these pieces. Not only will this save time on the initial drafts, you can do the review process with the client all together, which will save considerable time as well.

• **Reduce revisions.** No matter how fast you write, if your client has 7,688 rounds of revisions, you will end up making less than you would have working at the drive-thru down the street. The trick is actively managing the revision process. See my tips in chapter 11 on how to reduce revisions throughout the project.

• **Aim for some longer pieces.** I've focused mainly on how to turn out shorter pieces quickly, but when it comes down to it, it takes time to project manage each blog post no matter how quickly you write. So, while this isn't exactly a tip on how to write faster, it's important to mention that you can also dramatically improve your hourly rate by adding in some longer pieces to your projects as well. Yes, the 500-word blog posts are easier to find, but by mixing in both, you can increase your overall earnings in the long run.

Payoff: If you increase your writing speed so that you are able to write one additional blog post a week at $350 in the same amount of working hours, then you earn an additional $18,200 per year.

(!) **Build Your Business:** Pick one (or more) of the above suggestions to work on actively increasing your writing speed. You should aim to be able to regularly complete a 500- to 700-word blog post with one interview or web research in under three hours.

KEY TAKEAWAYS:
Increasing Your Income

• Set your income goal and know how much you need to earn each week/month to meet your goal.

• You can increase your hourly rate and have more billable time by writing faster drafts, while not sacrificing quality.

• Drop your lowest-paying clients to have time to find a higher-paying client.

• Always ask for more money when negotiating with clients.

• Periodically raise your rates with existing clients.

Section 5: Build a Business You Love

When people talk about the benefits of freelancing, the flexible schedule and the ability to work in your pajamas are usually the first things that come up. While those things are awesome, I personally think the biggest benefit is the ability to completely build your business in whatever way works best for you—everything from who you work with to what you write about to when you work.

It's so easy to just take the fly-by-the-seat-of-your-pants approach to building your business and just make it work. But I think the real trick is to take control of your business and build something that you enjoy, love and are proud of. There is something incredibly empowering about knowing that you have built an entire business and are supporting your family through your words. And even more so when you're creating a business that you love.

Chapter 16

Design Your Perfect Business

I had my best year ever in 2017. Yes, I earned my highest amount of money ever. But honestly that is not the main reason why I consider last year my most successful year as a freelancer. It's easy to focus on money. It's tangible. We need it to pay our bills and have a warm place to sleep. And it's a common benchmark for success. But it is really only part of the story when it comes to building and growing a successful freelance content marketing business.

The main reason that I consider it my best year ever is that I finally feel like I ran my business in the way that worked best for me. And for me the most important part is that I really liked all my clients—as in would love to have coffee or drinks with them. I really think that liking your clients is one of the most important parts of building a business that you love.

Over the past few years, I have really thought about changes I need to make so that my business works best for me personally as well as uses my strengths (and minimizes my weakness) so I can have happy clients. Here is how that looked for me this past year:

• I really liked all of my clients and felt that they were very nice people.

• I took six weeks of vacation and worked part-time for several other weeks when the kids were home.

• I mainly succeeded at taking one complete day off every week. Because I have teens, I work sporadically after 2 p.m., so I often willingly work on the weekend to catch up when they are busy with their own lives.

• I finished the first draft of a book based on my blog, which you are reading now.

• I wrote personal profiles for a mental health magazine. I really enjoyed writing these articles and especially enjoyed getting emails from the people I profiled, sharing that they loved what I wrote. You simply don't get that type of gratification in B2B tech.

• I met a lot of new and interesting people, including other writers and new clients.

• I helped many writers increase their income and satisfaction as a freelancer through my blog and free coaching calls (which any writer can ask me about).

• I was able to refer out about $70K worth of work to other writers over the year, which makes me very happy.

• I began using FreshBooks for invoicing and tracking income. My previous accounting "system" involved hoping everyone paid me, depositing all my earnings into one account and adding it up. It feels awesome to have a real system and be organized.

What Matters to You

But what's really important is what matters to you. Find a quiet hour or so to sit down and really think about what your best year ever would look like.

As you are envisioning your best year ever, don't think about how to make it happen or if it's possible to make it happen. That's another step I am going to help you with. But you can't have your best year ever if you self-edit yourself before you get the words out. Now is the time to be idealistic and think about how your business would look in a perfect world. Here is what I want my next 12 months to look like professionally:

• Continue to work only with clients who are very nice people and are creating great content.

• Continue to refer work to other writers from leads that come from my website.

• Publish and promote my book so that more content marketing writers can have businesses that make them happy and meet their financial goals.

• Continue to speak at writers' conferences and also begin speaking at content marketing conferences.

• Write and publish several personal essays.

• Continue writing personal profiles for the mental health magazine and look for new opportunities to tell people's stories, both in content marketing and journalism.

• Take six weeks of vacation.

• Stop working at 5 p.m. except for personal writing projects.

• Take at least one weekend day off completely from work, including personal writing projects.

• Continue doing free coaching calls for any writer who asks.

• Continue to refer overflow work to other writers.

• Continue writing about B2B tech but try to focus on clients where the content focuses on how tech affects and helps people.

• Continue to use FreshBooks as my accounting system.

• Figure out a way to track expenses that works for my scattered brain so doing my taxes doesn't require migraine medicine and a few bottles of wine.

• Make at least $100,000, preferably earn $120K to $150K and a stretch goal of $170K.

Odds are your perfect business looks very different. And that's okay. Actually, it's more than okay—it's the point. Yes, it doesn't happen overnight, but you have to believe in yourself that it is possible to create the perfect business for yourself. And it's very unlikely that you will get there unless you can clearly articulate exactly what you want.

However, it's a moving target. Because sometimes when we get what we thought we wanted, we realize that we were wrong. But often that's the best learning experience. Not to mention that our personal circumstances are constantly changing and that in order to fully take advantage of all the benefits of freelancing, we have to keep tweaking our business. So it's okay if you don't know exactly what you want for the rest of your working life. Just design your business so it works for you right now and for the next 12 to 18 months.

Here are some questions to help you figure out what matters to you and then design your perfect business:

• If you are currently freelancing, what is working well for your business? What do you consider the highlights of the past year?

• Which projects are you most looking forward to in the next 12 months? If you are new to freelancing, what would be your ideal projects?

• Describe your ideal client. Think both in terms of professional and personal characteristics.

• If you are currently freelancing, do you like all of your clients? Can you get rid of those you don't like?

• What personal writing projects do you want to start/finish in 2018?

• Is there a type of writing/publication/client outside of your niche that you would like to write for this year for variety and personal satisfaction?

• How much vacation time do you want to take?

• What type of networking (both potential clients and writers) feels most authentic to you?

• How many hours do you want to work each week/month? How are those hours ideally structured?

• Is there a day or time of day where you want to be unplugged from your business?

• How much money do you want to make? Write down a goal for how much money you need to pay the bills, how much money you would really like to earn and then a super stretch goal.

(!) **Build Your Business:** Make some time to sit down in a quiet place and answer the above questions in writing. Don't think about your answers or edit them based on what you think is possible. Write down the pie-in-the-sky dream. For example, if you think it's not logistically possible to take weekends off, but you really wish you could, write it down. Put your list away for a day or two to give yourself some space from it.

Picking Your Top Three Priorities

Building a business takes time and effort. But building a business that you love takes a lot of effort and creativity as well. To get there you have to figure out how to turn your perfect businesses into a reality. But you can't have everything at one time. Or you will likely compromise on everything or just give up.

Instead of jumping in the pool with all your clothes on, which is my natural reaction, start small and build from there. Pick two or three priorities from your list and figure out how to make those happen. The next two chapters will give you some practical ideas, especially in terms of writing about topics you care about and using the flexibility of freelancing.

(!) **Build Your Business:** Pull out your notes about your perfect business and reread through each one carefully. Circle two or three things that are most important to you and brainstorm ways to make each one happen.

KEY TAKEAWAYS:
Design Your Perfect Business

• You have the power to design every part of your business—hours, clients, type of writing, niche, outsourcing—in a way that works for you.

• Your perfect business will not (and should not) look like another freelancer's business.

• Don't try to overhaul your entire business overnight. Pick three priorities to start.

Chapter 17

Writing about Topics That Matter to You

The first thing I remember writing was a poem about the sunset while sitting on the vinyl seat of my parents' '68 gray Oldsmobile Cutlass. I was five. As my mom and I pulled into the grocery store parking lot, we were surrounded by the most beautiful deep purple and gray tones swirling in the sky. I told my mom I had a poem "bursting out of me" and I couldn't go inside the store to get ground beef for the casserole she was making. I had to write it down right that minute or I was going to explode into a million pieces.

My mom went against her better judgment and locked me inside the car with a pencil (I actually think it was an eyeliner pencil she found at the bottom of her purse) and the back of an envelope. It was the first time I ever had the sensation of not actually forming or creating words but just transcribing what was already in my heart and mind. And yes, I have a copy of the poem. But I really wish I had the original written in my little kid scribble.

I always knew I would be a writer. It isn't just something I do, but who I am. It's how I communicate with others when I'm mad. It's how I solve my problems. And it's how I share when I'm overjoyed. I never remember actually making the decision to be a writer, and I think that's because it was just always a given to me.

But I'm pretty sure that when I told my second-grade teacher that I was going to be a writer, I wasn't thinking of whitepapers on the Internet of Things or blogs on how to prevent ransomware from attacking your hospital's network. But that's what I spend most of my days writing about. Because you know, there just aren't a lot of outlets that are going to pay me to write about sunsets, no matter how beautiful they are. And I'm a grown-up with a mortgage and kids heading off to college in fewer years than I have fingers (wow, that's a scary thought). So I write what pays the bills. But at the same time, I want to stay true to the five-year-old sitting in the front seat of the car on the warm Florida evening.

Pay Your Mortgage Versus Pay Your Soul

Writers often tell me that they don't want to go into content marketing or do more content work because they went into journalism to make a difference and don't want to spend their days making money for companies. I totally understand this. And they are right. However, it is very hard to earn a good living these days writing only "save the world" journalism stories, except for a few very high-profile writers and authors.

The answer for me has been to try to find stories where I can make a difference when possible. But no matter how hard I try, that is not likely to be all of my client work. What has worked for me is to put my projects into two buckets: Pay-My-Mortgage stories and Make-a-Difference/Feed-My-Soul stories. These phrases keep the image of the brown-haired girl in pigtails writing the poem about the sky in my head. And most importantly, makes me take the effort to seek out the Feed-My-Soul stories, because those don't usually just fall into my lap.

I have learned (the hard way) I am much happier when I try to find Pay-My-Mortgage stories that are very interesting to me. I personally don't find lifestyle stories interesting, but how technology is being used in our daily lives is fascinating, as is the new technology being developed. It energizes me, even if it is for a company making money. And by referring to them as Pay-My-Mortgage stories, I remind myself that I can't work without a roof over my head.

By taking high-income stories that are less fulfilling, it also gives you the money to make a difference in our world in ways other than your words. It might be giving money to a local charity. Or having the time to volunteer during the day at your kid's school. Perhaps earning more money in less hours through content writing gives you the time to spend with your aging parents or teens who will be heading off on their own in a few years. We don't like to talk about it, but money gives us choices, and that's not a bad thing.

Taking high-paying, less-fulfilling content projects also gives us more freedom to take on lower-paying writing projects where we can make a difference with our words. Maybe it is writing for a local newspaper or taking lower-paying but higher-profile website work. For me it's writing my blog, which I absolutely love and would spend my whole day working on if I could. Other writers I know use the time to write fiction or a nonfiction book that is calling to them but has less commercial appeal.

⊙ **Build Your Business:** What projects are you currently working on that feed your soul? Think about what types of projects have been fulfilling and meaningful to you in the past.

Pitching Journalistic Stories to Feed Your Soul

Many freelance writers have told me that content marketing just doesn't feed their soul in the same way that journalism does. For years, I kept trying to find the answer in content marketing. While there are definitely projects out there where you can make a difference, I finally realized that the answer is actually journalism.

A few years into my freelancing career, I landed a gig freelancing for the local section of the Raleigh *News & Observer*. I am positive that I had some of my favorite moments ever as a writer as part of that gig: My front-page story on the police turkey drive that led to record-breaking donations, meaning that my words literally helped put food on the table; getting an email that a woman had refound her faith after attending a church event I wrote about; and talking with the families from Flight 93, which crashed in Shanksville on 9/11. I ended up giving up the gig because of newspaper budget cuts and higher-paying gigs taking my time. But I missed making a difference and sharing people's stories. So last year, I began writing profiles and reported stories for a mental health magazine. The difference in my overall mood and attitude towards work is remarkably better when I take the time to write stories that are meaningful to me.

So if you are worried about content marketing not being as fulfilling as journalism, remember that content marketing doesn't have to be all or nothing. And I really think that doing some journalism on the side is the right answer for many writers. Think hard about what will make you the happiest and most fulfilled. And what will help you honor your own version of your younger self writing about the setting sun.

(!) **Build Your Business:** Make a list of journalism outlets that you would like to pitch. Carve out time every week to spend an hour or two crafting pitches for publications about stories that are meaningful to you.

Finding Content Marketing Projects That Feed Your Soul

All of that to say, I do think that there are ways you can also find meaningful stories within content marketing. Some examples that I've worked on include a program at software company SAP that hires IT professionals with autism (CA Technologies), an article about using wearables, similar to a Fitbit, to help special needs kids (Hewlett Packard Enterprises) and a story about rescue dogs helping veterans overcome PTSD (Fifth Third Bank). Here are five strategies to finding stories that are meaningful and make a difference as a content marketing writer:

1. Look for companies producing journalist style custom publications. A few years ago, I wrote the most well-researched and meaningful article that I have ever written. It required 10 different interviews with top doctors at prestigious hospitals, was close to 2,000 words and will almost definitely make a difference in people's lives. And I was given pretty much journalistic freedom to report the story and take it where it needed to go. But it wasn't for a glossy consumer pub or even a nonprofit. It was for a custom publication produced by Fifth Third bank about treatment for life-threatening peanut allergies and was most definitely content marketing. Some companies are now producing journalistic-style publications for their customers and accept freelance submissions. It takes some research (and luck) to find these, but they are definitely out there.

2. Write for nonprofits. Many nonprofits are realizing that by providing content about the work their group is doing, they can increase donations and volunteers because people can put a face on the difference their group is making in the community. Some organizations write a newsletter while others need case studies and stories for their website. While the smaller local organizations typically don't have a big budget, many of the national nonprofits have the resources to pay market rates and have a strong need for great writers.

3. Limit the number of agencies and large companies you work for. While these types of projects typically pay well, I just haven't been able to find meaning working for huge corporations or through an agency. I will always have some of these on my client list because their names help me get other work and their budgets help me pay my bills. But I find that I am the least satisfied in my work when all of my projects come from these types of clients.

4. Work for companies with products or services that are helping people. Many companies are for-profit but are producing products or services that make a difference. It takes some creativity to see the impact and some research to find them, but I promise they are out there in pretty much every industry. A few years ago, I wrote landing pages for an online payment system that gives a portion of each sale back to charity. And I've written many case studies for a large technology firm about how their servers are providing broadband internet to people in rural areas and totally transforming communities and people's lives. On the surface, I would have thought writing about tech equipment was boring, but the case studies I worked on were some of the most meaningful pieces of writing I have ever done because the difference this piece of equipment made in people's lives was amazing.

5. Look for smaller and medium-sized companies with a passionate owner. I love working for companies that started with a great idea and are trying to compete with the big boys. I'm not talking about super small companies with no budget, but more in the 10–20 employee range who have a tangible product. I often find these companies in the tech field. There is something about the energy of a smaller company and knowing that your work can make a significant impact in their ability to provide more jobs and retain their current employees. Yes, the impact may not be as great as some of my other ideas and the money usually doesn't compare, but I personally find companies with a brilliant idea and a passionate owner to be very fulfilling to work with. I am usually viewed as a part of the team and can see how my words make a difference to the company and the employees.

ⓘ **Build Your Business:** Brainstorm ways that you can find content marketing projects that are fulfilling and meaningful to you. Every time you start a marketing push, make sure to keep this goal in mind.

Giving Back through Your Writing

Another option to feed your soul as a content marketing writer is to take gigs for free or at low pay where you can give back. I'm not a fan of free, but I think that when you are doing it as a volunteer for reasons other than money, then it can be a really important part of building a business you love. Here are a few types of projects that I have heard other writers taking for reasons other than money, such as to feed their soul:

• **Offer to write content marketing deliverables for a nonprofit organization that you care about.** Often providing a service is even more important than money. Nonprofits can benefit from personal profiles, newsletters and even blogs. Many times, writing the stories of those who benefit from the organization helps raise additional funds, which enables the group to help even more people. If you have experience with grant writing, you can also volunteer to help them earn grants needed for funding.

• **Help a friend or family member who is starting a business create effective content.** Now that you understand the value of content marketing writing and how it can help a business, use your skills to help a company that you believe in grow their business. Yes, it is still helping a business, but if it is for a person you care about or a product you believe in, then it can still be a project you feel passionate about.

• **Freelance at the local newspaper to spread the word about positive things in the community.** More than anything I have done, I feel that I have made more of a difference writing my articles for the newspaper, both features and my church column. I have helped raise money for a police memorial with a story on fallen officers, written about a group helping grieving widows and found homes for a dying woman's pets. And several of the businesses I wrote about were close to closing when the story was published and they ended up surviving due to the publicity.

• **Mentor a newer writer.** Yes, it's not the same as investigative journalism, but helping someone else get started is hugely gratifying. One of my surprises since I became a freelancer is how generous other writers are. I have been on the receiving end more times than I can count and find helping other writers to bring a satisfaction that writing about technology just doesn't have.

• **Start a blog about a topic that you care about.** Many writers have told me that writing for themselves is the most fulfilling thing they do. If there is a topic you feel passionate about and an audience that needs your information and perspective, start it yourself. It doesn't have to be something that helps grow your business, but something that gets you excited. It could be about animal rescue or ADHD or organic gardening. While my blog is about content marketing, I honestly enjoy every minute I spend writing mine and often put it over paying work because I love helping other writers.

(!) Build Your Business: Brainstorm ways that you can give back through your writing. This is only something that you should do if you feel called. I know many writers who use their many other talents to volunteer and keep writing as their business.

KEY TAKEAWAYS:
Writing about Topics That Matter to You

• Try to remember why you became a writer and make sure that you honor your version of the sunset poem.

• Make sure you have both Pay-Your-Mortgage and Pay-Your-Soul projects.

• Pay-Your-Soul content marketing gigs do exist—you just have to look a little harder.

• Consider pitching stories to journalistic outlets for your Pay-Your-Soul stories.

Chapter 18

Work Only with Clients You Like

The first few years of freelancing, I took any client who would pay me a decent rate. But after a few years, I realized that I get very stressed when I work with jerky people. And when I am stressed, I am more likely to give into the urge to binge watch whatever I am currently addicted to on Netflix, which needless to say, doesn't help my bottom line. Not to mention that no one—other than my dog, Katie—likes being around me in this state.

But on the flipside, when I work with people that I really enjoy and feel a part of a team, my productivity is off the chart. And I'm a nicer person. My family even likes me again. The difference in myself and my business when I work with nice people is really dramatic.

So probably about 2014, I made the "No-Ahole Rule" meaning that I would not work with anyone who was an ahole. I started screening my clients more and the minute I got a gut feeling that client was a jerk, I either didn't take the project or didn't work with them again. I wasn't very good at spotting the jerks from the beginning yet, so this mainly involved not working for clients a second time. My stress level went down, my productivity went up and my income followed.

I quickly had a full dance card, a few anchor clients and a steady income. So I took my rule a step further—I would only work with nice people. I learned pretty quickly that there is a big gap between not being an ahole and being a client that I genuinely liked. After a few tries, I figured out how to distinguish who was "very nice," and likely to turn into long-term clients and most importantly, friends.

I thought it would hurt my income, but the opposite happened. I made more money. And I was happier. Much happier. I honestly think that this is the biggest reason I broke six figures for the first time in 2015. This one decision changed my entire life and my career.

This meant never taking a client without having a "get to know you" phone call. And it meant turning down well-paying work. But it was worth it. Originally, I thought it would be hard to tell who was very nice in a 30-minute phone call, but I developed a screening process. If the phone call felt like an interview, then it wasn't a fit. Even more, if the client didn't have the time or desire to get on the phone with me before the project, then it wasn't a fit. But if the conversation flowed naturally and was comfortable then the client passed my "nice" test and I would usually take the project.

Over the next two years, I started being booked up most of the time and having little availability. I had to say no to potential new clients and referred them to other freelancers. But I realized that I could always make room for a well-paying client that I got along well with and worked well with. I simply told them my rule. I explained that I had gotten to the point in my career that I was able to pick who I worked with. I told them that when I first started to get some success, I made the no-ahole policy and then it progressed to the "Only Work with Nice People Rule." This was a huge jump because there is a big difference in someone not being an ahole and being a nice person. But I have gotten even pickier and have the "Only Work with Very Nice People Rule."

If a client is a good fit for me, then at this point they are usually laughing and always chiming in with "Oh my goodness. I totally agree. Life is too short." Or even better, "I have the same rule and wanted to talk with you to make sure you were very nice before we hired you." And if a client doesn't fit my personality and what I'm looking for, then there is a bit of uncomfortable silence and they don't know what to say.

Now your criteria is likely not exactly the same as mine. But that's the important part—finding out how to screen your clients so that at the end of the day, you are only working with clients that you genuinely like. I personally consider this the biggest marker of a successful freelancer—not income, not household brands, but the ability to choose your clients so that you only work with people that you'd like to go out to coffee with.

Just like everything in this book, that doesn't happen overnight, but the point is to actively know what you are looking for and be as selective as you can based on where you are in your career. At the beginning, I could only afford to turn down clients that were aholes. But even taking that first step made a really big impact on my personal and professional life.

Start by Being Yourself

I used to spend a lot of time trying to write, act and talk like I thought people expected of professional journalists and content marketing writers. It was hard work. It was uncomfortable. And it didn't really work. I was passed over for many more gigs than I landed and when I did land a project, it turned out to not be a good fit for me more often than not.

I couldn't figure out why. I was following all of the rules and doing everything the way the experts said to. But it wasn't working. Not to mention that I was miserable freelancing.

Then one day, I forgot about a potential client call until my phone rang. And since the client was in San Jose, it was 7:30 p.m. my time and I'd already partaken in a glass of red wine with dinner. I wasn't drunk by any means, but I was definitely much more "myself." I laughed during the call. I let my Southern mannerisms slip out (yes, y'all is a real word). I got really excited and started coming up with a bunch of new ideas for the client. It was a really fun call. And I even followed up with an email filled with emojis to the head of marketing for a major company.

Then the next morning I woke up and decided that I had completely blown what could have been a great client. I shouldn't have laughed. I shouldn't have used y'all. I shouldn't have told him how to do his marketing better. And I definitely shouldn't have used emojis. I was so mad at myself.

I thought those things until I checked my inbox and found that he had responded to my email—and offered me a very lucrative retainer gig. He commented that he enjoyed our conversation and he thought I would fit in perfectly with the rest of his team. The note even said that he wanted to talk more next week about my ideas. And I almost fell over when I saw that he had used a smiley face emoji in the email. The client went on to be one of my anchor clients and was a turning point in my career. I was happy, no, thrilled, but I didn't realize exactly why I had gotten the gig.

A few weeks later I was on another potential client call and I was deep into my act of acting like a formal and very professional corporate writer. It was going terribly. The client and I weren't connecting. I was trying to be super professional and I wanted to poke my eyes out. As a last-ditch effort, I decided to drop the façade, but this time without the assistance from a bottle of Chianti. I simply stopped acting like I thought I was supposed to and decided to let my personality shine through. Within a few minutes, the tone of the conversation changed and the client and I began connecting. Yes, I landed the client.

I don't think it was the laughing or the Southern slang or the emojis that made the difference. But instead the fact that I was letting my true personality show during the calls.

Before that moment, each time I acted the way that I thought clients wanted me to act, one of two things happened:

1. The client didn't hire me at all. I was stiff and boring. Even with great clips, I didn't give anyone a compelling reason to hire me. And I definitely didn't stand out from the pool of writers.

2. The wrong clients hired me. Clients who wanted a very formal writer who simply showed up to write would hire me. But ultimately since that isn't my personality or style or strength, then it didn't work out. These clients were not looking for a writer with a lot of ideas who wanted to be a part of a team, which is the kind of writer I actually am.

But when I started being myself, I was attracting the exact type of clients that were looking for my strengths (ideas, friendly, hardworking, a bit silly) and willing to overlook my weakness (the occasional typo). Previously, I had worried that if I let my personality shine then some people would not hire me. I was 100 percent correct but I was missing the bigger point. That was actually a very good thing because it weeded out the clients who were not ever going to turn into long-term clients to begin with.

It's so easy to get hung up on the details of freelancing. Is my LOI perfect? Am I in the right niche? Am I undercharging? Yes, those things are important. But ultimately, in my opinion if you are willing to be truly yourself in every part of your business—website, LinkedIn profile, About Me, LOIs, phone calls and follow-ups—all of the other things will work themselves out. I found that the instant I started being myself and letting my personality shine through, I began landing more clients and keeping more clients for years. And most of all, I began really enjoying my job.

(!) **Build Your Business:** Think about the clients that you really enjoy and make a list of their characteristics. Next think about how you can spot these clients in a phone call. Maybe it's a story like my no-ahole rule. Maybe it's a characteristic you look for. Or perhaps something totally different. It should be what's important to you personally and professionally.

KEY TAKEAWAYS:
Work Only with Clients You Like

- Develop a screening process for clients that works for you.

- Remember that you are interviewing the clients as much as they are interviewing you.

- When you are true to your personality, then clients who are likely to be a match will be attracted to working with you and those that are not a match will likely be not interested.

Chapter 19

Use Your Freedom

As my kids neared school-age, I was a huge ball of stress trying to figure out what to do. The plan had always been for me to be at home when they were little and then find a job when they went to school. But I realized that I didn't want to be tied into someone else's schedule. The freedom of freelancing was the main reason that I started freelancing instead of going back to work at IBM or another company.

With two kids, three dogs, a husband that travels and an elderly mother-in-law, someone has an unexpected need pretty much every week. And I never know when school is closed for a week due to two inches of snow (yes, this really happens in North Carolina), a kid needs an ice cream date with me after a tough week or my mother-in-law needs me to take her to a doctor's appointment. From the beginning, I used the flexibility to react to the things that happened, but it wasn't until a few years into freelancing that I realized I could also use the freedom to proactively set my own schedule.

One of the biggest benefits we have is the freedom to set our own schedules, which means working when we want as well taking time off when we want—in theory, anyway. It's easy to get so caught up in meeting client deadlines and finding new clients that we do not always take advantage of the flexibility. Yes, it takes planning. Yes, it takes sticking to your guns. But if you don't do this, then you will find yourself reacting to your clients' needs and getting burned out.

Building Time Off into Your Income Goals

The most common reasons freelancers tell me that they can't take time off is that they can't afford the time without income and that they can't simply shut down their business because their clients depend on them. The secret to being able to afford to take the time off is to build it into your weekly and monthly income goals so that you are making up the difference in income. But spread throughout the year, it doesn't seem painful or noticeable. It's when you try to make it up after the fact or all at once—been there on both accounts—that you end up crying at 1 a.m. (Wait, maybe that's just me.)

For example, at the beginning of each year, I decide how much money I want to make that year and then break it down into monthly and weekly goals so I can stay on track. Instead of dividing the annual goal by 52 weeks in the year, I divide it by 44 or 46 weeks depending on how long I plan to take off. I then put the extra money earned each month into a separate account to fund my time off. You can do the same to "pay yourself" during your vacation weeks. It is stressful to try to make up an entire week or two incomes in a month or two, but it is hardly noticeable when you spread it over the entire year.

Picking the Flexible Schedule That Works for You

I used to not really take advantage of the flexibility because I didn't have a set plan. I just tried to swing everything as it came. And that didn't work for me. I never took time off and was always working. In some ways I think it's harder to take advantage of the flexibility while doing content marketing writing than journalism. The reason is that when pitching publications, you can simply pitch less or stop pitching during the time you want to take off. But with content marketing, you are much more likely to have anchor clients that depend on you for a certain amount of work each week or month. Here are four different ways to make use of the flexibility of being a freelancer:

Taking Set Hours Off Each Day. One of the main reasons that I freelance is so that I can spend time with my kids after school. For the past nine years I've been freelancing, I've taken them to and from school so I have several hours in the afternoon that I'm unavailable for work. Once they are home, I will work if they are doing homework or hanging out with friends but I try to be available to hang out or take them somewhere. I know other freelancers who take time off from work most mornings to work out as well. They simply block this time out as they would a standing meeting with a client.

Whenever I sent out requests for interviews or a potential client asks my availability, I respond with the sentence "I am unable to speak every day from 2 to 4 p.m. EST, but can be available after 4 p.m. EST, if needed." This sentence has worked well and also keeps people from scheduling after 4 p.m. unless there is a reason. Yes, most people know that this means I'm picking up kids and I am fine with that. If a client becomes a long-term client, then I always eventually share that I really try to not have calls during that time, but if there is no other way then I can arrange to have my kids ride the bus. I've always had a positive reaction to sharing this and, honestly, if someone isn't okay with that, then they really aren't the type of person I want to work with regularly anyway.

Taking a Day Off Each Week. This has never worked for me, but I know other writers who have done this with great success. I think that this could work pretty well during the summer since it's relatively common to take Friday off. For me, I find taking one day off almost harder than taking two weeks off, but that might be my own issues at play. I think if you take this approach, then you have to either work more hours the other days or take on less client work.

The trick is simply saying that you are unavailable if someone suggests meeting on a Friday. You don't have to say why and you don't have to explain your reasons. "I have a conflict," "I am booked," or "How about Monday?" are all good answers to keep the day open. The less you say, the better. And the less exceptions you make, the easier I am betting it is to make this happen week after week.

Working Less During Certain Time Periods. I have a freelance friend that acts in local plays and she doesn't work very much when a show is going on. I try to work less during the summer months and school vacations. The trick for me has been deciding beforehand which clients I have to keep going throughout the summer and make sure that I make time for those obligations. And then I cut back on extra projects and new assignments during that time period. I try to work the minimum that I can to keep my business going and my mortgage paid.

Taking an Extended Vacation

I shut my business down typically twice a year for at least two weeks. For me, it's the only way to truly relax and I am pretty selfish about these vacations. After writing a whitepaper while my family explored Kauai, I no longer do any new work—no exceptions—while on vacation. No matter the money. No matter how much the client asks. No matter anything. Yes, it means that I have to turn down assignments and yes, it means that the week before I leave is usually filled with many early mornings spent writing and late nights spent finishing things up.

A freelance friend of mine takes off seven weeks every year and simply doesn't work. She does all of her work that will be due for regular clients before she leaves and lets them know that she will be gone. Then she shuts off from electronics and focuses on her family. While she may occasionally answer a client question or do an easy revision, she doesn't really work much at all. Her clients are happy to have the work in early and her business is still there when she plugs back in at the end of the summer.

I've taken an extended vacation about 10 times now and have learned a lot of lessons the hard way:

Decide ahead of time how plugged in you will be and if you will work while on vacation. I tell clients that I will not be doing any writing on the projects and that I will "try" to check email every few days, but that sometimes connectivity is a problem. I share that I am willing to answer any questions or do any urgent revisions if needed on vacation. I only work with sane clients that are typically very nice, so if they ever ask me a question on vacation it is usually something that only I can answer.

Start talking about your vacation about two months ahead of time. By sharing your vacation dates with your existing clients WAY ahead of time, they have plenty of notice and are usually very accommodating. I also start telling any new clients that I take within two months of my trip about my planned time off as well so that there are no surprises later. I usually send a reminder to clients about three weeks before the trip and then about a week before I leave.

Just say no. The only way to really take a vacation is to turn down work. If a client (either new or old) offers me work before a vacation, I ask if it is something that can wait until I get back. Sometimes it is. Sometimes it isn't. But if I can't REASONABLY fit it into my schedule before I leave and it can't wait, then I have learned that I have to decline the project. And when I waver on this, which I always do, then I just remember how awful I felt that day in Hawaii sitting alone in the condo. When possible, I try to refer the gig to a fellow freelancer because I feel less guilty turning it down if I am helping someone else.

Take your vacation adjacent to a holiday. The past two years I have taken the first two weeks of December off. So basically, when I get on the plane, I have shut my business down for the year because when I return most people are heading out of town. Both years, I have worked a little bit when I got back, but usually it was because I wanted to or the money was too good to turn down. This worked fabulously and gave me about four weeks of much-needed down time. I have also had success vacationing around Easter and July 4, mainly because many of my clients take time off around these dates so work tends to be slower.

Give your clients fake vacation dates. The first time I shut my business down to go to Costa Rica for 10 days, I told everyone that my last day of work was the day before I left on vacation. This was a terrible idea. I ended up writing posts on creating effective webinars on the flight to Costa Rica and having to find Wi-Fi as soon as we landed to send in the copy. Never again. I now give myself a buffer of a few days before I depart and a few days after I arrive back home. This way I have a buffer for the last-minute "client emergencies" as well as getting myself (and family) ready to leave.

Tell your client where you are going. Yes, some writers will say this is too much information. But I have found that clients are much more likely to respect my vacation if I share that I am going somewhere far away. My long-term clients almost always turn into friends, so it seems natural to share as well. So I tell them, "I'm going to Hawaii" or "I'm going to Italy" or "I'm going to Australia." I have had much better luck taking vacations that sound expensive and exotic than taking time off to go to the beach closer to home. You know, next time I go to the beach for a week, I might just tell everyone I am going to Antarctica or New Zealand instead, so no one contacts me.

KEY TAKEAWAYS:
Use Your Freedom

• Build vacation weeks into your income targets.

• Consciously build a schedule that works for your life

• Vacations are important. Your clients and work will still be here when you come back.

• Set parameters before you go about what type of work you will do on vacation.

Conclusion

There is a lot of advice in this book. And hopefully you've already started seeing the results of some of the ideas. If you haven't already joined us at the The Freelance Content Marketing Writer Facebook group, head over there now and join the conversation. And be sure to sign up for my newsletter so you get my latest blog delivered to your inbox at jennifer-gregorywriter.com/blog.

When I was first starting out, I wanted someone to tell me exactly what to do to be a successful writer. I was convinced there was a formula—a right way to do this. But I have realized that isn't 100 percent possible. Yes, I know that seems odd after you have just read an entire book. I've given you a crap ton of ideas and strategies. But it's up to you to turn those ideas into your very own business.

At the end of the day, you are only going to be successful if you build your freelance business specifically for you—your strengths, weaknesses, personality and goals. I run my business a little differently than my writer friends, and that's the way it should be. Look at others to get ideas and inspiration, but make sure your business is authentic to yourself.

It won't happen overnight. It won't happen next week. But if you don't give up, you will get there. When it feels like you are a fraud and that you are never going to land work, remember that every single freelance writer feels the same way—All. The. Time. I felt like it yesterday and probably will again next week. It is simply part of being a writer and a human.

Other writers are earning $100 or more an hour. Many writers will break six figures this year. And a handful will even earn $200K. There is absolutely no reason why you can't achieve the same thing. It could be the next email you send or the next event you attend that changes your career. But you will never know if you don't keep marketing and moving forward.

You've got this. I promise.

Acknowledgments

S tarting from as early as I can remember, I told anyone who would listen that I would write a book. Like from the time I could write. For years, my plan was to write a story that had something to do with horses. And then as I got older, it was about people who rode horses that fell in love with each other and lived happily ever after on a horse farm. Then somewhere in my mid-teens, my drafts and dreams were just about falling in love. I even had a title—*Heat Lightning*—after the silent Florida summer storms. Yes, really. And even worse, I'm secretly thrilled that by writing the previous sentence that my beloved title is actually in print, even if it's not on the cover.

But then I became a professional writer. I realized how much work it was to write a book. And how much you put yourself and heart out into the world with a book. So I decided that I absolutely positively was *not* going to write a book, no way, no how, never, not me. This went on for years. And I actually got in arguments with writer friends about how I was never going to do it. Even last summer, I was still adamant that I wasn't going to write a book.

But my blog readers and friends (especially Stephanie) and family (especially my sister and husband) kept harassing me to turn my blog into a book. So I wrote this book. And oh my goodness, it was a lot more work than I expected. But it was also more gratifying than I expected. I will even admit that when I finished the first draft sitting alone in a hotel room in Austin that I cried and cried because the words and message finally felt like they were from my heart.

But during the many winter weekends I spent writing it at my kitchen table, I often wondered if five-year-old Jennifer would have approved that my first book was about content marketing. She probably would have made a face. Then perhaps rolled her eyes. And then spouted off a retort that my book was supposed to be about love.

But in many ways this book is about love.

It's about how I built a business that I truly love. It's about how I've made a living doing something that I love. It's about how much I love helping other writers and seeing people support their family using their words. But also, this book (and my writing career) wouldn't exist without the love and support that so many people have shown me both in the freelance community, friends and family. In many ways, my entire career and life have been a group effort and I wouldn't have it any other way.

To my test readers, Pamela DeLoatch, Stephanie Vozza, Margaret Buranen, Alma Smajlovic and Sanyal Swati: Thank you so much for taking the time to read this book and give such helpful feedback. You gave me the confidence to keep going.

To all of my blog readers, you mean so much to me. And your encouragement is the reason I wrote this book. I have enjoyed getting to know so many of you through emails, comments and phone calls.

To my most longtime and loyal blog readers (and commenters), Holly Browne, Alma Smajlovic and Lori Ferguson: There are so many times I thought about quitting the blog in the early days and your comments kept me going. Lori, your consistent Twitter posts have brought me so many new readers.

To my editors and designer, Jennifer Lawler, Peggy Nehmen and Linda G. Hatton: I really appreciate your hard work and feedback. I couldn't have done this without you. Linda, I still stand by my opinion that starting 43 sentences in this book with the word So is the perfect balance.

To all of my freelance buddies through ASJA and FLX: I am so glad that our paths crossed through freelancing. You have made this journey so much more fun and I have learned so much from each of you. You know who you are. I originally had names, but I knew I would forget someone and feel terrible. Each of you means the world to me.

To Cat DiStasio, my amazing Virtual Assistant. This book wouldn't have happened without you. I cannot thank you enough for your patience with formatting and editing. But even more, I thank you for everything you do every day to help me run my business. You save my sanity and I really appreciate you.

To Barb Harper, my fabulous editor. I am so thankful that you put up with me. Without your excellent editing and flexibility with my last-minute rush jobs, I could not be a freelancer. And yes, one of these days, I will actually send you a project without revising the ETA time at least 4 times.

To Liz Alton, you saved my sanity by helping me come up with a title. In a single sentence you described exactly what I wanted to say. I was very close to giving up finishing the book because I couldn't come up with a title. I am forever grateful.

To Wendy Helfenbaum, you are the best cheerleader. Thank you for all of your support with ASJA, my career and this book. You are a wonderful friend.

To Stephanie Vozza, I am so glad that I sat next to you in Chicago many years ago. I honestly don't think I would be anywhere near as successful with my business without your support and encouragement. You have no idea how much you have helped me through the ups and the downs (and the fire pit stories) through the last five years. And thank you for telling me that I had to write this book. It wouldn't exist without you.

To Blair Waddell Gunter, I pretty sure I wouldn't have survived junior high and high school without your friendship, love and support. You are actually the only person that would endlessly listen to me ready aloud my boring horse stories. And I'm so glad that we are still a part of each other's lives. Your encouragement throughout the past 30 years is one of the big reasons that you are now reading this book.

To my mother-in-law, Sharon Gregory, I am so glad you are my family. I always appreciate how you ask what I'm working on and support my writing.

To Denise Goforth, you are the best friend and sister in the world. Your support of this book and my career means the world to me. I am so lucky that you are in my life.

To my mom, Anne Patterson, thank you for leaving me in the car to write the poem about the sunset. And all the hundreds of times since that you have encouraged and supported my writing.

To my dad, Sam Goforth, thank you for making me figure out a way to make money from my love of writing. You taught me that it really is possible to do both and not to give up till I figured out a way.

To my dogs, Hank, Katie and Larry, I am pretty sure I couldn't freelance without your company. Throwing the ball to you,

Hank, seeming 45 million times an hour is the best stress break ever. And I will never cease to be amazed at how you are sound asleep until the minute I get on the phone and then start howling like lunatics.

To my daughter, Laurel, you are the most creative and interesting person I have ever met in my life. I can't wait to see the wonderful things you create. I think you are really amazing. You have both taught me so much about myself and life by watching you grow up. I am so proud to be your mom.

To my son, Trevor, I am so proud of the kind young man you have grown into. You inspire me every day at how hard you work to achieve your goals. I love how passionate you are about your opinions and know it will take you very far in life.

To my husband, Trent, your love and support of both my writing career and this book means the world to me. Neither would exist without your encouragement. I love you and can't wait to see what the rest our life together brings.

First-Time Freelance Writer

Kickoff Activities

- Create a professional writer website with a detailed About Me section.
- Update your email signature to identify yourself as a freelance content marketing writer.
- Create (or update) your LinkedIn profile and include desired niches and any relevant work or volunteer positions.
- Ask any current or former coworkers or supervisors to write recommendations for your LinkedIn profile, highlighting relevant skills.
- Determine your target niches.
- Write an LOI for each niche.
- Have another writer review your LOIs and provide feedback.
- Create a list of local agencies in your area and state.
- Create a list of businesses in your niche that need your skills and expertise.
- Find local events both in marketing and your niche to attend.

Weekly

- Find contacts and emails for LOIs to send next week.
- Review job ads to find jobs that you are exceptionally qualified for and apply for them.
- Send emails to freelancer friends (if you know any), letting them know that you are looking for clients.
- Create and add to list of potential contacts, such as local business owners in your niche, friends of friends, former classmates, etc. Keep a list of all LOIs you send, so you can follow up.

Daily

- Do 5 to 10 marketing activities each day, including LOIs, job ads, following up with LOIs and connecting with former clients or coworkers who have moved jobs.

First-Time Freelancer with Related Career Experience

Kickoff Activities

- Define the niches you want to focus on.
- Update your LinkedIn profile and include all desired niches.
- Update your email signature to identify yourself as a freelance content marketing writer.
- Ask any current or former coworkers or supervisors to write recommendations for your LinkedIn profile, emphasizing relevant skills.
- Update the About Me section of your website.
- Write an LOI for each niche.
- Have another writer review your LOIs and provide feedback.
- Create a list of local agencies in your area and state.
- Create a list of businesses in your niche that need your skills and expertise. Include your personal network when you think about potential clients.

- Find local events both in marketing and your niche to attend.

Weekly

- Find contacts and emails for LOIs to send next week.
- Review job ads to find jobs that you are exceptionally qualified for and apply for them.
- Send emails to friends letting them know that you are looking for new clients. Tell friends who are also freelancers as well as those who work in other industries and positions.
- Search online for former coworkers and clients who have moved jobs to see if any of them might be in a position to hire a freelance writer.
- Create and add to list of potential contacts, such as friends who have moved jobs, coworkers, sources, industry connections.
- Create and add to list of all LOIs you send, so you can follow up on them.

Daily

- Do 5 to 10 marketing activities each day, including LOIs, job ads, following up with LOIs and connecting with former clients or coworkers who have moved jobs.

Writers with Journalism Experience

Kickoff Activities

- Define the niches you want to focus on.
- Update your LinkedIn profile and include all niches.
- Update your email signature to identify yourself as a freelance content marketing writer.
- Ask any current or former coworkers or supervisors to write recommendations for your LinkedIn profile.

- Update the About Me section of your website.
- Create a portfolio on your website and include any clips relevant to your chosen niches.
- Write an LOI for each niche.
- Have another writer review your LOIs and provide feedback.
- Create a list of local agencies in your area and state.
- Create a list of businesses in your niche that need your skills and expertise.
- Find local events both in marketing and your niche to attend.

Weekly
- Find contacts and emails for LOIs to send next week.
- Review job ads to find jobs that you are exceptionally qualified for and apply for them.
- Send emails to freelancer friends letting them know that you are looking for new clients.
- Search online for former coworkers and clients who have moved jobs.
- Create and add to list of potential contacts, such as former clients who have moved jobs, coworkers, sources, industry connections.
- Keep a list of all LOIs you have sent, so you can follow up on them.

Daily
- Do 5 to 10 marketing activities each day, including LOIs, job ads, following up with LOIs and connecting with former clients or coworkers who have moved jobs.

Experienced Content Marketing Writer Wanting to Grow Your Business

Kickoff Activities
- Define the niches you want to focus on.
- Update your LinkedIn profile and include all niches.
- If needed, update your email signature to identify yourself as a freelance content marketing writer.
- Ask any current or former coworkers or supervisors to write recommendations for your LinkedIn profile.
- Update your website with any new clips.
- Write an LOI for each niche.
- Have another writer review your LOIs and provide feedback.
- Create a list of local agencies in your area and state.
- Create a list of agencies that specialize in your niche.
- Use the Audience First Method to brainstorm businesses needing your experience
- Find local events both in marketing and your niche to attend.

Weekly
- Find contacts and emails for LOIs to send next week.
- Review job ads to find jobs that you are exceptionally quali-fied for and apply for them.
- Send emails to freelancer friends letting them know that you are looking for new clients.
- Create and add to list of potential contacts, such as former clients who have moved jobs, coworkers, sources, industry connections.
- Keep a list of all LOIs you have sent, so you can follow up on them.

Daily

- Do 5 to 10 marketing activities each day, including LOIs, job ads, following up with LOIs and connecting with former clients or coworkers who have moved jobs.

About the Author

Jennifer began her career working as technical writer and earned a Master's Degree in Technical Communication. When her youngest kid went to school, she started her own freelance writing business. Over the past 10 years, she has written for many national clients including IBM, Apple, Adobe, Samsung, Allstate, Salesforce, State Farm, American Express and Costco. Her work has also been published in Entrepreneur. com, *SUCCESS* Magazine and TheAtlantic.com. She also worked as a freelance reporter for three years for the Raleigh *News & Observer* newspaper.

She is a Florida native and didn't see snow until she was 21 years old. She now lives in North Carolina with her husband, two teenagers and three very spoiled dogs.

Dear Writers,

Thank you for reading *The Freelance Content Marketing Writer: Find Your Perfect Clients, Make Tons of Money and Build a Business You Love.* I really hope that my book has given you some new ideas on how to build your freelance business and helped you know that you are not on this journey alone.

While this is the end of this book, I'm still writing more advice, tips and the mistakes that I make along way on my blog at **jennifergregorywriter.com/blog**. I hope you will visit and subscribe so you can get my new posts sent straight to your inbox.

You can also interact with other readers and post questions on my Facebook page at **facebook.com/JenniferGoforthGregory**.

If you have questions or need someone to brainstorm clients, niches or marketing ideas, send me an email from the contact tab of my webpage.

I offer free 30-minute phone calls to any writer who asks. I don't offer paid coaching so I'm not going to sell you anything. Many writers have helped me along the way and I like to give back. Plus, it's always fun to make new friends.

When you have a success story—land a new client, hit an income goal, break into a new niche, find a marketing trick that's working for you—send me your success stories. I love to share these stories on my blog to help inspire other writers.

—Jennifer

Made in United States
North Haven, CT
01 November 2022

26208600R00153

Kathy